One-Piece Flow vs. Batching

A Guide to Understanding How Continuous Flow Maximizes Productivity and Customer Value

Endorsements

K25855 – *One-Piece Flow vs. Batching* by Charles Protzman

"This is the first book I have read that comprehensively confronts the ills of batching in a single volume and provides an alternative. It does so in language that is clear and accessible to all levels in an organisation - from CEO to middle managers to workers on the shop floor! A great contribution to the 'improving productivity' agenda. Read it!"

Augustus J. Lusack MSc, MBA,
Lean Six Sigma Black Belt,
Founder: 'Why Not?' Solutions Limited,
www.whynotsolutions.co.uk;
Head of Pathology, Northampton General
Hospital, Northampton, UK

"This book is relevant to both newer students of Lean as well as seasoned Lean practitioners looking to gain an insightful understanding of a cause of much waste in our organizations, BATCHING. By presenting numerous examples from many different industries, readers will finish the book appropriately armed to first identify and then eliminate batching."

Kenneth W. Place
Lean Six Sigma Master Black Belt
University of Illinois BIS

"I am a batch-person. Whenever there is a chance to batch I have a certain tendency to do so. Charles Protzman's book made me reconsider this position. I think this is the best one can say about any book. As a 'good' scientist I do not agree in all points; but I consider the arguments brought forward for one-piece flow convincing. It is *not* a dull repetition of you 'should not batch', but reasonable arguments against batching are developed. While this sounds not very exciting, practical examples and great writing style make it a very enjoyable read. In short - the authors successfully continue Ohno's quest towards one-piece flow."

Matthias Thürer
Professor, Jinan University, China

"I have spent 38 years in the steel industry in quality assurance, process control and operations management and have been successful by finding ways to optimize performance by taking advantage of new technology, understanding and controlling process variation, and looking for opportunities to get more for less. Like the plant manager that Charlie dedicated this book to, though, I have to admit that I still believe that in some industries there is cost savings to be had by increasing batch size. I would be the last guy to tell you that it might be efficient to make a heat of steel for each casting that you are producing. But I will admit the book makes you think about what savings could be possible if that was technically possible.

Charlie uses an example in the book of having to wait until you fill up the dishwasher and run the cycle before you get a clean plate. He challenges you to imagine if there was a dishwasher that does one place setting at a time. What a dumb idea, right? I was just in an innovation class where it was discussed that Whirlpool has been working on just such a device, but has not yet overcome the resistance to the cost of retrofitting it into current households. Their new strategy is to work with builders of new homes. Maybe not such a bad idea after all. If we stick to our old paradigms we may never see the opportunity to try something different.

Remember there are three stages to implementing change. The first stage is total resistance. When the idea first comes up it is always a really dumb idea. Giving up on economies of scale and our very nature to complete one task on all parts before moving on? After enjoying an easy read with some great examples and taking advantage of the workshop activities that Charlie has presented, you might make it to stage two in the change process: 'hey this stuff may actually work'. When you actually implement one-piece flow and watch your inventories disappear, your quality improve, and your costs decrease you will have made it to stage three in the change process. You will be proud to tell Charlie, 'I am glad I thought of it'."

Jon Schumacher
Chief Operating Officer Wheel, Amsted Rail

One-Piece Flow vs. Batching

A Guide to Understanding How Continuous Flow Maximizes Productivity and Customer Value

Charles Protzman

Joe McNamara

Dan Protzman

CRC Press
Taylor & Francis Group
Boca Raton   London   New York

CRC Press is an imprint of the
Taylor & Francis Group, an **informa** business
A PRODUCTIVITY PRESS BOOK

CRC Press
Taylor & Francis Group
6000 Broken Sound Parkway NW, Suite 300
Boca Raton, FL 33487-2742

© 2016 by Charles Protzman, Joe McNamara, Dan Protzman
CRC Press is an imprint of Taylor & Francis Group, an Informa business

No claim to original U.S. Government works

Printed on acid-free paper
Version Date: 20150923

International Standard Book Number-13: 978-1-4987-2694-8 (Paperback)

Visit the Taylor & Francis Web site at
http://www.taylorandfrancis.com

and the CRC Press Web site at
http://www.crcpress.com

This book is dedicated to a favorite plant manager of mine who happens to work in China. He has done an exceptional job of turning around his plant in his first two years, but his success is also inhibiting his ability to truly maximize his profitability.

He doesn't know it, but he inspired this book. I have worked hard to convert him from the batching mindset to one-piece flow but, as of this writing, have not succeeded in converting him. Hopefully by the second or third edition, if we are that fortunate, we will have converted his thinking to that of a flow mindset. But only he can change his mind. No one else can do it for him. All I can do is hopefully provide a compelling need for him to change. Hence the writing of this book.

Contents

Foreword

The core idea of one-piece or continuous flow is to maximize customer value while eliminating waste. Simply put, it means creating more value for customers using fewer resources. An organization dedicated to flow-based processes understands customer value and focuses its key resources on value-added activities. The ultimate goal is to provide perfect value to the customer through a perfect value creation process that has zero waste.

I am a one-piece flow practitioner. I have found in my experience that batching is the largest enemy of any organization that wishes to implement flow-based processes. If you happen to be an OPF practitioner as well, you also know this to be true. But, do you know the root cause of waste?

The authors of this book give you the answers. From the perspective of "Batching," "Flow," and "Bumping,"* they take us on the journey that will help you understand the root causes of batching and how it connects to the eight wastes.

This book will ask you to participate and engage your mind, and it will try to help you "wrap your mind" around the key issues. Chapter 5 contains an example of pen assembly using simple mathematical reasoning. It is obvious to us that

---

* Bumping is explained in much more detail in *The Lean Practitioner's Field Book*, Protzman, Kerpchar, Whiton, Lewandowski, Grounds, Stenberg © 2015 CRC Press.

batching is the antithesis to one-piece flow, and wherever it can be avoided, it should.

You will learn the authors' proven results from a wide array of examples in the field, confirming that one-piece flow is much better than batching. In the first example alone, through-put time, after a one-piece flow "kaizen," was reduced by 25%. Cycle time dropped from over 21.05 seconds to 15.8 seconds. (The risk of rework was minimized dramatically as well.)

So, why do people batch? The authors give us eight well-explained reasons. I could not agree more with the authors on the reasons, especially their first reason, which is our minds. Human beings evolved from our hunting and gathering ancestors to a new age of agriculture. In ancient times, people were always facing the crisis of food shortages. So, the answer was to use batching to deal with the worry of future shortages. If we can fully understand all eight reasons the authors give us then we can take action accordingly, to the best of our ability, which will benefit you, the reader, by implementing your own one-piece flow system.

Why is batching the silent productivity killer? Batching causes a lot of negative things: quality issues, rework, longer lead times; it requires more space, more tracking information, more indirect labor; it creates a lower respect for people, worse on-time delivery, more inventory, and, finally, lower customer satisfaction as a result.

As stated earlier, I too am on the journey of converting from batching to one-piece flow, but I understand we cannot change from batching to one-piece flow overnight. So we take it in steps. Our first step was to re-layout our shop floor to a one-piece flow model. As a result, travel distance reduced by 22% (584 to 458) and WIP reduced by 48% (62 to 32); but ideally, in stage two, we can reduce travel distance by 76% (584 to 140) and WIP by 63% (62 to 23). Also, throughput time will reduce from ten days to four-and-a-half days. We improved a lot and will benefit more from the authors' recommendations in the future.

The authors state, "When you work on something you don't need, you can't work on something you do need!" This could not be truer!

How can we produce efficiently with limited resources? I believe the authors will convince you to try your best to minimize batching and create flow not only in your job but in your life as well. It will certainly be a big change if you decide to start on your one-piece flow journey, but once implemented, you will wish you started long ago, and if you have not started you will realize you can't afford to wait any longer.

Jordan Jiang*
Former CI Director
Chart Cryogenic Engineering Systems

---

* Jordan Jiang 姜殿泉 | CI Director 精益总监 has held multiple middle or senior level management positions for several companies. He has over 14 years of Lean enterprise/Lean manufacturing experience plus over 17 years of additional manufacturing/management experience. He has worked in Japan for more than two years, so he can fully understand TPS. Jordan's experience includes industrial and manufacturing engineering, operations, quality, total productive maintenance, supply chain management, inventory management, and logistics. Jordan is well versed in Kaizen Events, 3P, and A3 Thinking. Jordan has obtained dramatic results; he improved the Lean awareness of his employees and has created a Lean culture for many companies. Jordan holds his MBA from Fudan University of China. Jordan takes a hands-on approach and has helped customers to achieve results as good as saving the need for 70% of company space, reducing deficiencies per vehicle by 40% (1.01 to 0.6), improving production efficiency by 20% (HPV 9.6 to 7.7), reducing lead time by 80%, and many other significant improvements. Chart Cryogenic Engineering Systems (Changzhou) Ltd.|查特深冷工程系统 (常州) 有限公司, 388 West Hehai Road, New District, Changzhou, Jiangsu | 213032 | China | 中国 常州 河海西路388号, Direct: +86 519 8596 6000 ext. 6012 | Mobile: +86 15866779718.

Preface

The purpose of this book is to help people realize what batching is, the fact it is all around us, and how it affects us, not just in our business lives but in our personal lives as well. This book is also designed to support anyone involved in continuous improvement (CI) activities and help provide a compelling need to change and overcome the resistance to implementing flow and, in particular, one-piece flow processes, whether it be in the factory floor or in the banking office.

A process has an input and an output where either a value-added or non-value-added activity takes place in between. Every process, whether it is on the shop floor or in the administrative setting, can be improved. However, there is always one thing lurking behind the scenes and always working against us; we call it the Silent Productivity Killer!

This book attempts to argue the problems associated with this silent productivity killer, which is our inextricable need to utilize batching processes. We also help to provide some insight into why all of us, no matter what the activity, always feel the need to batch.

We will provide you, the reader, with some concrete arguments as to why batching, while sometimes necessary, is never the most efficient solution for most processes and why flow, especially one-piece flow or continuous flow, should always be our ultimate objective when driving for increased productivity in any process. One-piece flow is the way to conquer this silent productivity killer—that is, batching. It is our hope that other researchers continue to further explore and provide additional understanding of this topic.

One of our goals was to make this book interactive while leaving the level of interaction up to the reader's discretion. We have included what we call timeouts for the reader to reflect and answer questions or provide their own input prior to moving forward. The idea is that when you are done reading you will have a notebook of sorts, with some actions that hopefully will be beneficial on your journey to converting to one-piece flow. It is not imperative that everything is filled out in order to gain a full appreciation of this work, but we hope it will help enhance your understanding of this silent productivity killer and provide you with your own personal action plan to conquer it.

Acknowledgments

We would like to thank

- MaryBeth Protzman for her detailed edits to the entire book.
- Ken Place for reviewing a later draft of the book and his constructive and insightful comments on the overall flow.
- Dr. Matthias Thürer* for his technical comments on the first draft of this book and his contributions to content.
- Jordan Jiang for reviewing the first draft and providing the foreword to this book.
- Meg Protzman, McDaniel College math and science major, for letting me include her note.
- Andy McDermott for reviewing an early draft of this manuscript.
- Augustus J. Lusack† for reviewing an early draft of this manuscript and for his revision suggestions.
- Mike Meyers, president of MPM Business Consulting Group, formerly assistant general manager at Magna Donnelly, for reviewing a later draft and contributing some of his experiences to the book.

* Dr. Matthias Thürer, Jinan University, matthiasthurer@workloadcontrol.com.
† Augustus J. Lusack MSc, MBA, Lean Six Sigma Black Belt, founder of 'Why Not?' Solutions Limited, www.whynotsolutions.co.uk; Head of Pathology, Northampton General Hospital, Northampton, UK.

- Mike Hogan, Progressive Business Solutions, who was the Lean consultant, and Shawn Noseworthy, who was the director. Both led the successful transition to one-piece flow in the hospital nutritional services example in the book.
- Dr. Steve Klohr, Paul Akers, and Norman Bodek for providing content to the book.
- Steve and Julie Stenberg for their contribution referencing article on simultaneous publishing.
- Mike Bland, senior project engineer, Amsted Rail Co. Inc., for inspiring the section "Will people pay more for one-piece flow."
- Leslie Gilbert for her critiques of the later draft of the book and suggestions for content on batching in the education world. Ricardo van Snek, MBA, from the Netherlands, for his review and last minute edits to the book's first pages.

Authors

Charles Protzman, MBA, CPM, formed Business Improvement Group (B.I.G.) LLC in November 1997. B.I.G. is located in Baltimore, Maryland, and specializes in implementing Lean thinking principles and the Lean business delivery system—LBDS. www.biglean.com

Charles is the coauthor of the following books and research papers:

- *Leveraging Lean in Healthcare: Transforming Your Enterprise into a High Quality Patient Care Delivery System*, recipient of the Shingo Research and Professional Publication Award.
- *The Lean Practitioner's Field Book: Proven, Practical, Profitable and Powerful Techniques for Making Lean Really Work.*
- *Leveraging Lean in the Emergency Department*, Recipient of the Shingo Research and Professional Publication Award.
- *Leveraging Lean in Surgical Services: Creating a Cost Effective, Standardized, High Quality, Patient-Focused Operation.*
- *Leveraging Lean in Outpatient Clinics: Creating a Cost Effective, Standardized, High Quality, Patient-Focused Operation.*

- *Leveraging Lean in Medical Laboratories: Creating a Cost Effective, Standardized, High Quality, Patient-Focused Operation.*
- *Leveraging Lean in Ancillary Hospital Services: Creating a Cost Effective, Standardized, High Quality, Patient-Focused Operation.*
- *The Silent Productivity Killer: Understanding the Negative Consequences of Batch Dependent Processes to your Business.*
- *The Lean Practitioner's Field Book: Study Guide.*
- *COBACABANA (Control of Balance by Card Based Navigation, An Alternative to Kanban in the Pure Flow Shop*, Dr. Matthias Thürer, Dr. Mark Stevenson, Charles Protzman ©2014. See www.workloadcontrol.com.

Charles has over 34 years of experience in materials and operations management. He spent 13 and a half years with AlliedSignal, now Honeywell, where he was an aerospace strategic operations manager and the first AlliedSignal Lean master. He has received numerous special-recognition and cost-reduction awards.

Charles was an external consultant for DBED's Maryland Consortium during and after his tenure with AlliedSignal (now Honeywell).

He had input into the resulting world-class criteria document and assisted in the first three initial DBED world-class company assessments. He is an international Lean consultant and has taught students courses in Lean principles and total quality worldwide.

Charles spent the last 18 years implementing successful Lean product line conversions, kaizen events, and administrative business system improvements (transactional Lean) all over the world. B.I.G. was a strategic partner of ValuMetrix Services, a former division of Ortho-Clinical Diagnostics, Inc., a Johnson & Johnson company. He is following in the footsteps of his grandfather, who was part of the civil communications section of the American occupation. C.W. Protzman Sr. surveyed over 70 Japanese companies in 1948. Starting in late 1948, Homer Sarasohn and C.W. Protzman Sr. taught top executives of prominent Japanese companies an eight-week course in American participative management and quality techniques in Osaka and Tokyo. Over 5100 top Japanese executives had taken the course by 1956. They then invited Dr. Deming (their second choice after Dr. Shewart) to Japan to follow up on quality improvements with the Japanese. The CCS course set the stage for the "economic miracle" in Japan. Many of the lessons we taught the Japanese in 1948 are now being taught to Americans as "Lean principles." The Lean principles had their roots in the United States and date back to 1436 with the Venetian Arsenal* and later to Taylor, Gilbreth, and Henry Ford in the early 1900s. The principles were refined and expanded by Taiichi Ohno at Toyota® and supported by the "P" course taught by Dr. Shingo to thousands of Toyota and other Japanese engineers. Modern-day champions are Norman Bodek, Jim Womack, and Dan Jones.

Charles participated in numerous benchmarking and site visits, including a two-week trip to Japan in June 1996, where he worked with Hitachi in a kaizen event. He is a master facilitator and trainer in TQM (total quality speed), facilitation, career development, change management, benchmarking, leadership, systems thinking, high-performance work teams, team building, Myers–Briggs Styles indicator, Lean thinking, and supply chain management. He also participated in Baldridge Examiner and Six Sigma management courses. He was an assistant program manager during "Desert Storm" for the Patriot missile-to-missile fuse development and production program. Charles has his BS and MBA from Loyola University

---

* *Venetian Ships and Shipbuilders*, Lane © 1934 Johns Hopkins Press. We assume many of these principles go back to the ancient Egyptians BC and the Romans, but have no proof as such.

in Baltimore, MD. Charles is also a member of SME, AME, IIE, APT, ASQ and the International Performance Alliance Group, an international team of expert Lean practitioners http://www. ipag-consulting.com.

Joe McNamara is president and chief executive officer of McNamara Holdings, which include TTarp Inc.

Joe McNamara was formerly the vice president of Global Operations of ITT Control Technologies based in Valencia, CA. Prior to being vice-president of Operations, Joe was general manager of ITT Heat Transfer in Cheektowaga, New York. He led the introduction of Lean Six Sigma into the $400 M, ITT Fluid Handling Division as Six Sigma Champion with 12 Six Sigma Black Belts in the United States and Canada. Outside of work, Joe enjoys spending time with his wife, Karen, participating in ultra-marathons, and reading.

Joe is a certified Lean manufacturing master and Six Sigma champion. He received a BS in mechanical engineering from University of Notre Dame, Indiana, and an MS from the University of Pittsburgh, Pennsylvania. Joe has a PE license in the State of Pennsylvania.

Daniel Protzman, Director of Customer Solutions.

Daniel joined Business Improvement Group in 2014. With four years' experience in the health-care field, Daniel brings an interesting perspective to the company. Daniel's previous medical recruiting and staffing company went through a major series of transitions in his tenure, where he was able to help guide the company in a positive direction. He was a source of knowledge for the process improvement team and eventually left that company to follow his true calling in continuous improvement. Daniel is a certified MBTI practitioner and holds a bachelor's degree from Virginia Tech. Daniel focuses on networking and aligning our consultants with companies wishing to improve. He also spends time consulting in the field directly for clients. Outside of work, Daniel is an avid Crossfit enthusiast. For any direct questions or interest in service, contact him at danprotzman@biglean.com.

Chapter 1

The Silent
Productivity Killer

The "batching" of processes is all around us, every day, and is detrimental to all types of businesses whether they are in the services industry, government, health care, or manufacturing. These batched processes even kill productivity in our personal lives. How can we convey this concept to you? This book will explore the said "batching phenomenon," define what it is, show when and why it occurs, and prove how it lowers our efficiency and robs us of our productivity.

Imagine for a moment...

- You walk up to the counter in a fast-food restaurant and order a cheeseburger. The counter person says, "You will have to wait Sir/Madam, until we get 10 more orders for those, then we can start the next batch for you."
- You are driving in a taxi, and the driver tells you that you have to stop at each street until 10 other taxis arrive, then you all can move together to the next street.
- You click on "send mail," and the program tells you that you have to wait until there are 10 more emails in the queue before you can send yours.

- You are at the amusement park and are told, "Sir/Madam, you must wait until we get seven other people to fill up the car before we can send you."
- You go to the Japanese Steakhouse and are told, "You have to wait for 10 other couples to arrive before the chef will start."
- You go to the check-in counter at the hotel and are told, "Sir/Madam, you must wait until 10 other people arrive before we can check you in."

Any one of these situations would drive us crazy; they are all examples of batched processes. Rereading the list we instantly say, "Well two of them are fine"—the Japanese Steakhouse and the amusement park ride are real-life examples. These are just two quick examples of batched processes that have worked their way into our paradigm. Why do we accept these two examples but reject the others as ridiculous? These examples are what we refer to as *The Batching Mindset*, aka—"the silent productivity killer."

The Initial Source of Inspiration

Back in the early 90s Dave O'Koren, a colleague of mine, and I were conducting our first five-day Lean class at Bendix Communications (now Honeywell). During the class we asked employees to brainstorm the definition of world-class while we wrote their answers on a flipchart. We had just converted our first line to one-piece flow in the plant when one of the participants who had seen the new line yelled out, "Eliminate batching and go to flow." At this remark the class plummeted deep in discussion over batching vs. flow.

One of the participants simply couldn't comprehend and asked me why one-piece flow was better. I replied, "Because, as we had witnessed on our first line, it significantly increased our productivity (over 50%)." She retaliated with many reasons why batching was actually the more efficient way to do things and that sometimes you *had* to batch. At the time, I could not think of any better answer, and told her defiantly one-piece flow is always better than batching based on our experience and that, for now, she should just take our word for it. Of course I lost her for the rest of the week. As they say, if you win the argument, you will lose the customer.

We tried to convince her with some more examples throughout the week, to no avail. Why was this concept so hard to convey? It seemed so logical and simple to me, but I couldn't quite get it across to the others. Dave and I showed the rest of the class some batch vs. flow exercises and videos of the line we implemented, which, to us, proved it was much better compared to the batch environment they had before. After constant urging and communication we probably had convinced some of them, to a point, that one-piece flow was better; but I am sure they all still had their doubts. After all, I know some were thinking, "Well, it might work in the exercises, but those were designed to work … and it might have worked on the one line we implemented here at the site, but that doesn't mean it will work on every line." (This has been a very common objection in every class I've taught since then.)

For the past 30 years, I have been working on this problem of proving one-piece flow is better than batching and trying to understand why people always feel batching is always more efficient. It just happens to be a difficult concept for many people to understand, and even harder to embrace. My hope, when you are done with this book, is if I have not convinced you that batching is the silent productivity killer, that I will at least have made some traction toward that premise.

A good friend of mine, Ken Place,* explained it like this:

1. Most people really struggle with the idea of a process or a system. It is hard to think about optimizing a process or

_____
* Personal correspondence with Ken Place, 2/3/2015.

a system if you don't understand it. It is easy to optimize a step in a process or keep an individual busy. The result is local optimization vs. process or system optimization.

2. The whole need for the optimization of processes (Lean) is very new in our evolution. It used to be perfectly acceptable to wait in line a reasonable period of time or work to piece rate in a factory. The challenge now is that societies' expectations have risen so much, and competition is so plentiful, that we need to optimize (one-piece flow) just to exist as businesses.

3. I tell classes, "You do not have to *like* the fact that we must continue to get better every day. Hell, many times I don't like it. The problem is nobody is asking if you like it or not, it is happening all around us and around the world, and it will continue to happen whether you like it or not, so why not at least get good at it?" Adopting the ideas of one-piece flow is crucial to our company's survival.

What Is Batching?*

The word batch† comes from Old English, meaning "to bake" or "something that is baked." Even today we still bake things in batches; in our kitchens we make batches of cakes, brownies, and bread. After all, what sounds better than a freshly baked "batch" of cookies, muffins, or brownies? Yet, as good as cookies sound, why are we inclined to apply this batching concept to all aspects of our lives?

We define a batch process as, "where one operation is done to **multiple** parts prior to moving to the next operation." So, this means that one doesn't see the first completed piece until the entire batch, of whatever it is you are making, is completed.

---

* *Lean Practitioner Field Book*, Protzman, Kerpchar, Whiton, Lewandowski, Grounds, Stenberg © 2014 CRC Press.

† From Middle English bache (or bacche) < Old English bæcce ("something baked") < bacan ("to bake"). Compare German Gebäck and Dutch baksel.

A Brief Example of Batch vs. Flow

Let's walk through examples of batching (see Figures 1.1 through 1.3).

Figure 1.1 describes the basic concept of batching. This means that a batch, or lot, of parts is waiting for the first step or first operation (Op #1). One by one, the parts are processed through the first operation. After completing the first step we place them in a queue, i.e., storage location, where they wait for the rest of the parts or lot to be completed through Op #1. We call this a "lot delay" because they are waiting for the rest of the lot to be completed.

Figure 1.2 shows how parts being batched are moved through several operations. Again, each lot is processed through each operation, normally one at a time, and then stored while it waits for that step or operation to be completed

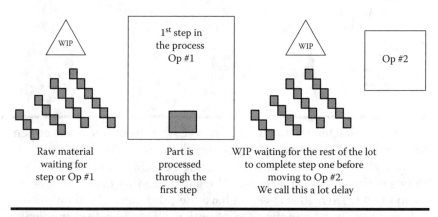

| Raw material waiting for step or Op #1 | Part is processed through the first step | WIP waiting for the rest of the lot to complete step one before moving to Op #2. We call this a lot delay |

Figure 1.1   Batching defined. In this example we show raw material waiting for the first step in the process. This is considered a raw material (RM) storage delay. The next step is to transport it to Op #1. This operation could be anything from drilling a hole in a part on a drill press to folding a piece of paper for a newsletter. Once the step or operation is completed for that part, we transport it to storage where it waits until we complete Op #1 for the rest of the lot or batch of parts. We call this a lot delay. Once all the parts are completed, they will move to the next step, which is Op #2. (Source: BIG Archives.)

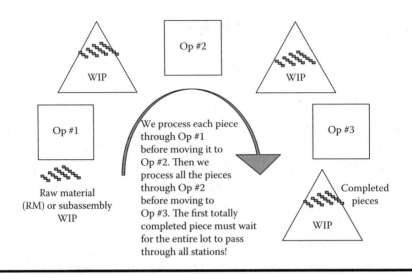

Figure 1.2   Batching defined. (Source: BIG Archives.)

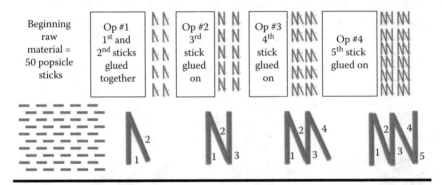

Figure 1.3   Batching defined. Let's say we have 10 sets of five wooden Popsicle sticks that we want to glue together. Operation (Op) #1 involves gluing the first two sticks together. Batching means that 10 sets of the first two pieces must be glued together prior to moving to Op #2. Then 10 sets would have the third piece glued on prior to moving to Op #3 and then Op #4 until we have 10 sets of the final result pictured above. One-piece flow would be doing each operation on one set until it is completed and then doing the same for the second set, etc., until all 10 are assembled. (Source: BIG Archives.)

on the rest of the parts in the lot. Then the entire lot is moved to the next operation and so on.

Figure 1.3 shows an example of gluing five Popsicle sticks together with instant-dry glue.

- The person batching will glue the first two sticks together for all 10 sets.
- They will then glue the third stick on, for all 10 sets, which is Op #2.
- They follow with the fourth stick for all 10 sets, which is Op #3.
- Then finally they glue the fifth stick for all 10 sets, which is Op #4.

Timeout 1

Just about all of us think this to be the most efficient way to do this task. *Wouldn't you agree?* List on your Timeout 1 sheet which Popsicle assembly method (batch or flow) you think is more efficient and why (see Timeout 1).

If the person performed this task as one-piece flow, they would assemble each set one at a time, through each operation. So they would pick up the first two sticks, glue them together, and then glue the third, fourth, and fifth until the first assembly was completed. Then, they would assemble the next set and so on until all 10 sets were finished. Which method do you think is quicker? Why?

Timeout 1 Review

If you picked the first example you will have a lot of company; about 99% of us would pick the first method. We will revisit this later to see if you still agree once you are finished with the book.

Timeout Exercise #1

- List below which Popsicle assembly method (batch of flow) you think is more efficient and why.

_____
_____
_____
_____
_____
_____
_____
_____
_____
_____
_____
_____
_____
_____
_____
_____
_____
_____
_____
_____
_____
_____

Hold on to this to revisit later and see if you agree once you are finished with the book.

If you picked the first example you will have a lot of company. 99% of us would pick the first method.

Chapter 2

Who Batches … and What's the Big Deal If It's "Me?"

We All Batch

This is the honest truth: we all batch, and we do it all the time. To paint a simple picture, have you ever made a "triple batch" of cookies? This is a good example of batching, because we are making one large batch consisting of three smaller batches of the same recipe in one bowl. Making cookies is already a batch process, but our thought concept is, "While I'm already making one small batch, I might as well make all of the batches at once in one large batch." We tend to think that continuing the same action multiple times, rather than completing one batch at a time, is much more efficient. In a factory, if we had three people each making a single batch at the same time, we would call this working in "parallel." Working in parallel is different than batching.

"So what's the big deal," you're asking, "I've made triple batches before and they've worked perfectly fine." But you have to agree—sometimes triple batching can lead to problems. Have you ever run into one of the problems below?

- Forgot to put in the salt?
- Put in too much salt?
- Put in too much sugar?
- Forgot to put in the baking soda?

Missing just one of these components can ruin the entire triple batch. The cookies will either taste flat, too salty, too sugary, or won't rise properly. Consider instead, if we had made a small batch. We could put the ingredients in a smaller mixer using a smaller bowl, mix them faster, and get them on the first pan and in the oven right away, before moving to the next pan. In some cases we may not even need a mixer; we could stir it just as fast by hand. Now if we forget or add too much of an ingredient we have only impacted a small batch vs. the entire triple batch. We notice problems faster, which allows us to react and correct those mistakes without affecting our entire product.

Consider, for a moment, the triple batch process. First, we need a much bigger mixer and mixing bowl and more space for everything we have to put on the counter. Then, we have to open all the ingredients and mix them all together, which will take longer than mixing a single batch recipe. Next, we lay out as many cookie sheets as needed, which happens to take up quite a bit more of our, sometimes limited, counter space. I don't know about your kitchen, but between the giant mixer, the mixing bowl, and all of those ingredients laid out, as well as all the big measuring utensils, I'm stacking cookie sheets where you wouldn't expect to stack cookie sheets. Now safety has become a problem … in my own kitchen!

So now we scoop the batter for each cookie, normally with a tablespoon, and place it in rows on each pan until we fill all the cookie sheets. Then we put the first two or three cookie pans in the oven. Usually this is the point where we start to feel satisfied; we are finally going to get a "finished product." However, do you realize that now the rest of the cookie sheets are waiting on the counter taking up space, not to mention being exposed to the elements? This is what we would call WIP, or work in process. Do you think this could impact the quality of our cookies? Better yet, relate this back to a process in your company—can you see quality problems becoming an issue in this example?

DING! Oven is done and now we need room to set out three cooling racks. (I wish I had been cleaning up to make room when those first cookies were in the oven.) We remove the cookie sheets from the oven, put them on cooling racks, and then put the next two or three trays in the oven. Stop and think ... was the first cookie we scooped the first cookie that went into the oven? It seems we've lost track of which cookie sheet we prepared first. Do you think this could get us into trouble in our businesses if we didn't keep track of the cookies?

Making a triple batch always slows us down from getting the first cookie in and out of the oven and in our mouths. It's likely, with our first small batch, we could be eating the first cookie before we even get the first pan of this "triple batch" into the oven.

Now is where we start looking at improving the process. What if we made them into an even smaller batch, like one-half the amount the recipe calls for? How long until we get to taste the first one? Would it be about half the time? What if we made it even smaller?

Would you believe cookies can even be made one-piece flow? While you shake your head no, think all the way back to the "Easy-Bake Oven" (see Figure 2.1). The size of the machine is smaller than our giant mixer, not to mention that it works with a simple light bulb. We make enough mix* for one cookie (which is very fast), put it into the oven on a very small pan, and have it in our mouths a minute or so later.

---

* It is a specially prepared cookie mix made by Hasbro.

Batching process: Triple batch of cookies

Mix the whole triple batch

Place mix all on pans first

Place in oven

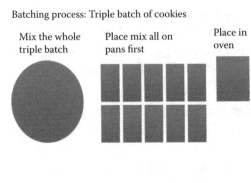

Disadvantages of batching
- Takes longer to get the first cookie
- Requires more space
- Requires a bigger mixing bowl
- More inventory is in the process

Flow process: Small batch of cookies

Mix

Place on first pan

Place in oven

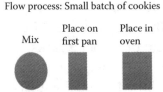

Advantages of flow
- Get first cookie faster
- Mix exposed to air for less time
- Requires less space

Easy-Bake Oven One-piece flow

Advantages of flow
- Get lots of cookies—fast!

Figure 2.1   Easy-Bake Oven by Hasbro. Cooks one piece at time using a simple light incandescent bulb vs. making cookies in batches. (From BIG Archives.)

If we made a mistake in our batter (which is much less complex now), when would we notice the mistake? "Yes, right after the first cookie!"

So how else do we batch? Let's talk about dishwashers. One can wash a couple of place settings by hand much faster than batching (loading, waiting, and unloading) the dishwasher. First of all, we have to rinse the plates prior to placing them in the dishwasher anyway, according to the manufacturers. They work great after a large party, but really the dishwasher is a place to store inventory/WIP while we wait for it to be cleaned. That first dirty cup could have a cycle time of a week, from when you first placed it in the dishwasher until you completely filled it a week later. What if we needed that cup sooner—How many of us would grab any dirty dishes we could find to justify running the dishwasher through a cycle? We are now waiting about an hour for it to be done. We could have instead grabbed the cup, washed it, dried it, and used it.

I'm not arguing the effectiveness of dishwashers or that they don't make our lives easier, but from an efficiency standpoint, there is a lot of waste in the process. Think back to the Easy-Bake Oven; what if we had a dishwasher that used minimal water and soap and had enough space for one plate or bowl, one cup, and one set of silverware, but washed it in a minute? Restaurants have dishwashers with 60 second cycle times that wash whole racks of dishes.

Golfing is another great example of a batching concept. Think about it. Most golfers play in foursomes. Each player goes to the first hole (Op #1). Then each player takes their first shot, and then they all move to wherever their balls landed and take their second shot (Op #2), sometimes by walking but normally by golf cart. Think about it ... if golfing were one-piece flow, we would not have foursomes. We would just have people play solo, through all 18 holes.

Sometimes golfers do play solo if there is no one to match them up with. You can get a round completed much faster if you are not waiting for three other golfers to tee off before you can continue to play. In fact you could probably complete your round in less than 2 hours. This is why a solo golfer or even a group of two golfers end up having to play through each foursome they encounter.

This leads us to the thought process that there are reasons, and sometimes very good reasons, why we batch. Why? Because playing in a foursome is more fun and social, even though it is less efficient.

Most golfers are not playing with the thought of being extremely efficient. Some will endlessly search for their lost ball, take 10 practice swings, plan out their putts with multiple strategies, or are just plain not ready for their turn. In these cases, golf rounds are now taking up to 5.5 hours in some cases. This is when you will hear avid golfers complain about "slow" people in front of them, especially if the slower players don't let them play through. Most avid golfers think about efficiency and want to get their round done in 3.5–4 hours.

They will drop a new ball instead of searching for a lost one, take one practice swing, line up their putt once, and are always ready to go when it is their turn.

The other problem with golfing is the starting process. Everyone is scheduled for a different tee time and starts at the first hole. But think about the "shotgun," i.e., parallel, starts. This is where all 18 foursomes start on one of the 18 holes at the same time. This is a more efficient way for the golf course to maximize its revenue. However, it is still batching three very large groups of 18 players through a 12-hour day (see Figure 2.2).

Another aspect to this golf analogy is the "best ball" method of playing. In this case each player plays from whoever has the best shot from the foursome. This method increases efficiency tremendously because it helps speed up the slower players and removes the impact of defects from the game, i.e., hitting the ball in the woods.

Since golfing is more of a recreational activity, we would assume most of us would have no compelling need to change. However, most of us really do care about being more efficient when it comes to everyday tasks, even to the point of being

Option 1: Traditional golfing—each foursome starts at the first hole—assume 4 hour rounds of play over a 12 hour day.

The first foursome is done at the end of hour 4 and then we get another foursome every 13.3 minutes. This works out to 144 players. In this model the first 17 holes sit idle for some period of time. i.e. 2nd hole is idle for 13.3 minutes but 17th hole is idle for 226 minutes. This pattern repeats as the last foursome finishes their rounds. This model would be more efficient if you didn't have to "dry" up the golf course each day.

Option 2: Shotgun starts 18 foursomes start in parallel, one on each hole—assume a 4 hour round of play.

In this option, we can get three batches of 18 players completed in our 12 hour day. This equals 4 players * 18 holes * 3 batches = 216 players. However, there are some pitfalls to this model. For instance, there is excess transportation for just about every foursome to get to their starting hole and get back to the clubhouse.

Figure 2.2 Golfing calculations.

somewhat resistant if someone suggests an improvement idea to us. To this day, I still find myself wanting to batch everyday tasks, and each time I do, I end up wishing I hadn't.

One day, last summer, I was working around the house planting bushes in a brand-new garden. So, naturally, first I dug all the holes. Makes sense, right? (see Figure 2.3). As long as I have the shovel in my hand, I might as well dig all 12 holes. Then I got each plant and set it next to the hole. Then I took the plastic container off each one. Next I put a little fertilizer in each hole. Then I went to plant the first one. Oops ... The hole is not big enough. So I had to go all the way to where the twelfth bush was going to be planted and where I had already dug the hole, about 50 ft away, get the shovel, and bring it back (another 50 ft) to the first bush. Then I dug and made the hole bigger (rework!). I tried the bush in the hole several times until it finally fit. But then I had to take it out again. Why? Because, while I was making the hole bigger, I was also shoveling out the fertilizer I had just put in the hole. What a waste! So I went back to the twelfth bush again (50 ft away) and got the bag of fertilizer and brought it back to the first hole (another 50 ft). Fortunately I had enough fertilizer. Otherwise,

Figure 2.3　Planting bushes.

I would have to make another trip back to the store. Have you ever done something like this? Be honest!

Then I planted the bush and shoveled back in the dirt. I had similar problems with other holes, which required me to move the shovel and add more fertilizer to each hole as I went. Finally, once they were all planted, I put the mulch around each one and then started watering them. The first bush was looking a little peaked since so much time went by before I started watering it. After I thought about it, I realized I could have been watering it while I was doing the second bush and then watering the second bush while I was doing the third. So in the end it took me quite a while and a lot of rework to get these bushes planted. But, who really cares? It's just an everyday task around the house. I'm off from work, and the last thing I want to think about is being more efficient. But, you know, it took up a large part of my day, and now other plans for the day had to take a back seat.

What if I had just done one bush at a time? Crazy, right? But think about it. I get the shovel and dig the hole with the bush right there. Now I can size the hole to the bush, which are all different sizes, and if it needs to be a little bigger, I already have the shovel there. Once the hole is the right size then I put in the fertilizer, the bush, and the mulch and start watering it. In the end I actually get the 12 bushes planted much faster doing them one at a time vs. the other batching method, and they are all watered immediately as I move on from one bush to the next. Which process is more efficient? I started thinking: I could have had time to get the rest of my plans done or even had time to take a nap!

In the business world, when we analyze processes, we look at them from both the product's (the bush) and the operator's (the person planting the bush) point of view. If you were the bush, which process would you like better? While this may sound like a really silly question, when we implement one-piece flow our first step is to become the product (the bush) or the thing being batched and then study it to see what happens throughout the entire process. Now this planting example above, while totally true, seems like a silly story; What could it possibly have to do with real life?

Let's take the emergency room* for an example of "real life." We, the patients, are now like the bush in the example above. We are the product. Just like the bushes, we find ourselves constantly waiting as we are batched through the entire process. First, we wait to see the nurse, then the registrar, then the doctor; we wait to take tests or x-rays, we then wait for results, and finally, we wait for the doctor to tell us what is wrong, how to fix it, and then to be discharged or assigned a room on the nursing unit. Because the process is batched, our length of stay is much longer than it needs to be. How many times have you had to wait hours in an emergency room to see a doctor, all the while in great pain?

Many hospitals and urgent-care centers are now moving to variations of one-piece or one-patient flow models where the time to see the doctor is decreased to 20 minutes or less.† Now, which method sounds better, flow or batching?

Batching occurs everywhere in our daily lives and in our business processes. Batching creates errors and defects, results in safety problems and clutter, and creates a constant demand for more space. It robs us of time, profit, and cash.

You will find you don't have to look hard to find batching. You just have to be able to stand in one place and watch ... really watch. Train your eyes to look for it and you'll see it everywhere—we certainly do. It occurs in most processes in our factories, offices, hotels, financial centers, government offices, sports, restaurants, and landscaping, construction, aerospace, automotive (still), and electronics. It's everywhere and it silently kills our ability to reach our highest productivity levels.

---

* See *Leveraging Lean in the Emergency Department*, Protzman, Kerpchar, Mayzell © 2015 CRC Press.

† *Leveraging Lean in the Emergency Room*, Protzman, Kerpchar, Mayzell © 2014 CRC Press.

Even as I am writing this book, I'm sitting here in my hotel room in Rotterdam,* watching the housekeeper strip the twin beds. She puts the bottom sheet on each bed then the top sheet on each bed. Next she puts on the comforters and, finally, the pillows on each bed. So she is batching the process. Not only is it taking her longer because of all the extra distance she is traveling, but what if I wanted to lie down? I can't lie down until both beds have gone through the entire process, which ends with her finally getting the pillows done and in place on each bed. The important thing to keep in mind about batching is how it affects the customer.

---

* Rotterdam is in the part of the Netherlands formerly known as Holland.

Chapter 3

Types of Batching

Types of Batching

Pure Batch

Pure batching is working with a "lot," or "group," of parts and doing each task to each part or product as a "group." For example, consider mailing holiday cards. We write notes on all the cards, then we put all the cards in envelopes, then we address each card, then, finally we stamp each card. Many times the cards get mixed up, fall off the table, or end up in yet another pile waiting for an address.

Most restaurants batch by table. They ask each person what they want to drink, then come back and pour water for each person while the bar is making up the drinks in a batch. Bartenders are also batchards (*more on batchards later*). If they get a drink order with six separate drinks, and three are the same, they will batch the three drinks (each step), and then proceed to make the rest of the drinks one-piece flow, and then they are all served as a final batch. Hence, a batch within a batch (see Figure 3.1).

Again, the server returns to take everyone's dinner order. A little bit later they finally bring the drink orders from the

Figure 3.1 Batching drinks. (From Shooters by Peter Griffin PDP-336-280-image. License: Public Domain. http://www. publicdomainpictures.net/view-image.php?image=19344&picture= shooters.)

bar. Then, they bring the starters/appetizers together, the salads together, then the main course, and lastly dessert and coffee. Since everyone's main course is not ready at the same time, someone's dish will inevitably end up under a warmer—or sometimes not, and it gets cold. What happens when your dinner order is not to your liking? Many of us refuse to send it back because our meal goes back into the queue, and by the time we get our "reworked meal," everyone else is already finished. Batching always creates problems, which are systemic to batching.

If it weren't for the etiquette of waiting for everyone at the table to receive their meal before eating, plates would be brought out one at a time in one-piece flow fashion as they were completed in the kitchen and ready for our consumption. Some restaurants now actually do this. Just imagine never getting a cold meal again, we could run the heat-lamp companies out of business. The heat lamps are just another example of applying minor repairs, or Band-Aids, to your process, instead of actually fixing the problem. China has a way around this problem. They have a different system. Most of their restaurants have tables with lazy susans. The dishes come out as they are prepared and are placed on the lazy susan. Then everyone eats family style. Hence, no batching.

Timeout 2

Think of a time you had to buy a special piece of machinery, like the heat lamp, to account for a variation or defect in your process, instead of removing the actual problem (see Timeout 2).

Segmented Batch

Segmented batching is processing a batch of products one piece at a time—for example, running only one model type down the line at a time and then converting the line over to run another model type. This would entail building all Toyota Camrys on the same line in the morning using one-piece flow, then building all Toyota Corollas on the same line in the after-noon, one-piece flow. In a machine shop it would be equivalent to running "like parts" for a day, or several days, in order to minimize setup times. Many times this can be an interim strategy for companies that aren't ready for, or will never pursue, nor feel they have a need to pursue, truly mixed-model one-piece flow production.

Cashier Line: Segmented Batch

This style is apparent in most retail stores (see Figure 3.2). Picture everyone standing in a line in front of each cashier station. All of a sudden the person in front of you doesn't have the bar code or RFID tag on their product. The cashier hits their "Andon" light or pages a manager, or anyone they can on the floor, for a "price check." Meanwhile, you are stuck behind this person, waiting, and you watch the people in the other line leaving ahead of you. Go ahead and raise your hand again if you've ever said to yourself, "I picked the wrong line."

Timeout Exercise #2

- Think of a time you had to buy a special piece of machinery to account for a variation or defect in your process, instead of removing the actual problem. List what it was and, if possible, how much it cost.

_____

_____

_____

_____

_____

_____

_____

_____

_____

_____

_____

_____

_____

_____

_____

_____

_____

_____

_____

Figure 3.2 Waiting in line. In the queue you are always at risk of being in the "slow" line. (From Public Domain. http://commons.wiki-media.org/wiki/File:Waiting_in_line_at_a_food_store.JPG.)

So what's the answer? One line feeding all of the cashier stations. Chances are you've seen it and didn't even realize it was a one-piece flow model. This model is in use at Best Buy, T.J. Maxx, HomeGoods, and Old Navy, and in some organizations such as banks and Disneyworld. In this model there is one line feeding all the registers. As soon as one register opens up, the store directs the customer via overhead speaker to the open register, i.e., "Register two is now open." This is similar to a model at most banks and airports. This model does, however, hide the waste of the slower cashier or problems any particular cashier may have (see Figure 3.3).

*Period Batch**

Period batching is working on a batch of things or tasks for a specified time period. An example of this might be in the

---

* *Design of a Period Batch Control Planning System for Cellular Manu100 yard during*, Riezebos © 2001 Print Partners.

Figure 3.3 Waiting in line. At Marshalls, T.J. Maxx, HomeGoods, Best Buy, Old Navy, and other retail stores they have fixed this problem by having each person wait for the next available cashier. (From Public Domain. http://commons.wikimedia.org/wiki/File:Waiting_in_line_ at_a_food_store.JPG.)

machine shop, where work is performed on one type of part on second shift and then other parts on first shift.

In a biotechnology company, it is typical for work to be done on one type of solution for 8 hours and then switched over and work is performed on another type for 8 hours. Traffic lights are like period batch. They batch traffic for a certain amount of time.

Location Batch: Kanbans

This is a new type of batching category we have created, due to the physical location of the products produced. For example, the product is forged in Building #1, then sent to Building #2 for machining, then sent to Building #3 for heat treat, and finally to Building #4 to be assembled.

We also see this whenever we outsource or subcontract to another location, where they are forced to batch up their products prior to shipping them. Even at Toyota in Kentucky, their subassemblies are built at other supplier plants. For instance, Dana Corporation would make the chassis, then ship it to Toyota in 2-hour intervals. In essence, kanbans are a result of

Table 3.1 Pros for Location Batching, i.e., Setting Up a Cell at the Customer's Facility

Pros for the Supplier	Pros for the Customer
• Creates "barrier to entry" for competition • Establishes a new location that can supply products to other customers as well • Provides a working model to use for other customers • Improves communication • Offers possible opportunity to supply other products to the same customer	• Lowers shipping costs • Reduces expediting fees (overhead costs) • Reduces inventory carrying costs • Reduces space needed to store inventory • Improves communication

Source: Authors.

the location batch designation, as they are used to link processes or companies together.

In a move to minimize some of this type of batching, many companies are moving their manufacturing "cells" or, in some cases, product lines right into the customer's plant (see Table 3.1).

At one company, this yielded the results listed below:

■ 52% increase in sales, and 40% sustained year over year sales growth with a significant increase in profitability. New marketing strategies implemented with focus on repeat business. Long-term agreements and kanbans in place with major customers, and recovered a customer that would not deal with them for three years.

■ Reduced setup times by over 70%, throughput time by 80%, and travel distance by 50%, resulting in a reduction of 8 to 10 weeks to 1 week quoted for lead time for repeat parts and 3–4 weeks for new parts.

■ Work in process (WIP) reduced by 75% and achieved 60 inventory turns on raw material.

■ Total productive maintenance program implemented and heijunka card scheduling system established.

- Vendor-managed inventory based on long-term price agreement established with steel supplier who delivered once a day and created a pull system from the finished goods kanban they created.
- 80% of operators are cross trained, certified operator program started.
- Selected as prime supplier for their customer and located a cell at the customer's plant.
- They had no layoffs and realized a 40% increase in perfect attendance.
- Air conditioning and hot water installed, health-care plan instituted, 401(k) plan instituted.

Process Definition

A process (see Figure 3.4) is anything with an input, which is then transformed into an output. An input starts with raw material from the ground or from the brain. It is then converted during the process to the output desired (or sometimes not desired, i.e., a defect). It can be physical or mental; it can

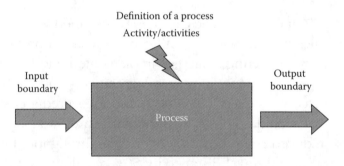

Definition of a process

Activity/activities

Input boundary

Output boundary

Process

Some or several activities may occur in the process box, and they may or may not be value-added. To be considered value-added they must meet three criteria*:
1. Physically change the part or mentally change the patient for the better
2. Customer cares or is willing to pay for that step in the process
3. The step is done right the first time

* Definition inspired by the AMA movie, *Time: The Next Dimension of Quality.*

Figure 3.4   Process definition. (From BIG Archives.)

be a manufacturing step for a product, or a series of manufacturing steps. It can be cocoa turned into hot chocolate, or hot chocolate processed further where milk and marshmallows are added to make it creamier, richer, and more delicious.

A process can be information, which is transformed into a different output by a particular input. When we take a patient's history in the emergency room we have an input of information from the patient, which produces the output, which is the beginning of the patient's medical chart.

Processes are everywhere; writing an email or text is a process. Writing and editing this book is a process.

Systems Thinking Definition

A system has an input and an output but is based on a collection of processes (see Figure 3.5). For instance, all companies share the order entry (OE) to collecting the cash process. The input is an order or demand for the product or service, and the output is the collection of cash for that service. Everything in between the placement of the order and collection of the cash is part of the overall system. There are two major systems available for this OE to collect process, batching or flow.

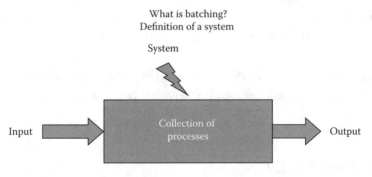

Figure 3.5   Systems thinking process definition. (From: BIG Archives.)

However, some processes may be hybrids with some of each. When we step back and look at the overall system and how to improve it, we call this systems thinking.

Types of Processes

There are several different types of processes. They range from batching to continuous flow.

- One-piece flow is adding each input sequentially to one part until it is completed.
- Batching processes add the same input to several parts in the first step in sequential order and then add a second input to each of the parts, but not necessarily sequentially, until the parts are completed all process steps.
- Continuous flow processes are one-piece or multiple-piece flow in parallel, where each input is added sequentially on an automated line. Continuous flow processes are generally high volume low mix or low variation, but can be high variation if setup changes are reduced to zero. For instance, a line that reads bar codes in order to change colors or composition of materials based on programming presets in the machines on the line.
- Lights-out (automatic) processes are one-piece flow continuous flow lines that can run unattended.

One-piece flow processes can handle high volume low mix to low volume and high variation if the lines are studied, designed, and run with standard work.

Batching Systems

Batching, as we said before, is always present and unconsciously lurking in the background, ready to disrupt one-piece flow practitioners at any time. It is important to remember to look at the overall systems, which are at work.

Where Do We Find Batching?

As stated earlier in the book, but we think bears repeating here: batching is prevalent in every company we visit all over the world. The batching paradigm is so strong within all of us, we find everyone, everywhere, batching all the time. Watch anyone working on two or more of something at a time, and you will normally see them utilizing a batch process.

Batching can be observed in all types of organizations: at restaurants, fast-food establishments, banks, insurance companies, government agencies, hospitals, airports, and traffic management. Batching occurs at the hardware store when making keys or by teachers preparing newsletters for school children, stores wrapping packages, or a company processing invoices.

Leslie Gilbert writes*:

> Thanks for the opportunity to review your book. Over the week that I've been reading through the chapters I have found my eyes opening to the many examples of batching that surround me—both at work and at home. I now 'see' batching EVERYWHERE! And seeing it is the first step toward improvement. Even as a lean practitioner, I found myself making excuses that batching is required under some circumstances but I didn't have the words to explain the 'why.' I now have a lengthy list of areas we batch in my margin notes of your book!! By the way, I did the paper airplane manufacturing exercise with a whole grade of our fourth graders and it was WONDERFUL! In this exercise, they make paper airplanes with 4 stations, making various folds and inventory is created because one station has more work than the rest. On the first pass, the exercise is run with a 'push' approach; every

---

* Based on email correspondence with Leslie Gilbert, Howard County Schools Continuous Improvement Coordinator, dated 2/15/2015.

station works as fast as they can, resulting in tons of inventory. Then we make the planes by batching three at a time and finally we run the exercise as a one-piece flow. The result is always more total units, better quality, and fewer inventory in the one-piece flow scenario, and the participants are often surprised by the results. The fourth graders totally understood the batch vs. flow concept (better than some of the adults who take the course!) Here's my current list of batching spots in various school systems that I've noticed:

- Carpool drop off/pick up (batch 3)
- Lunch Line
- Friday folders (like in the example you describe)
- Classrooms
- Ground equipment repairs just prior to lawn mowing and snow plowing seasons
- Pay checks
- Grading papers
- Technology purchases of large computer quantities
- Computer labs
- Public surplus sales

And many more … I believe the ultimate flow is computer-based learning at the pull of the student's understanding!

My daughter-in-law, Lauren Protzman, also a teacher, says, "I just have to batch my grading of papers. I am sure it's faster than one-piece flow. I just can't give that up. But, when it comes to putting furniture together, I totally get it. We were assembling IKEA dressers and while assembling the first one we batched the drawers. We had this huge pile of partially assembled drawers all over the room and I was getting cramps in my legs because I just couldn't move. Even the cats couldn't move. I got really uncomfortable and told my husband, JC, you have to finish a dresser so one of us can move in here. We finally got that one put together. Then when assembling the second dresser, we did one drawer at a time. I did the first part of the drawer, while JC finished it and put it in the dresser; kind of like a little assembly line. Then I would start the next one. We realized that the second experience was much more comfortable, efficient and pleasant." Laughing, she stated, "there was no screaming during the second one. However, I am still batching my grading of papers."*

Most firms batch the back-office or administration processes, including end-of-the-month closings, yearly budgeting processes, and accounting check runs. Even the US government has all personal tax returns due on April 15. This forces companies that do taxes to hire lots of temps for 3 months and then let them go or accounting firms to work overtime and weekends during "tax time." Think about it. What if our tax returns were instead due on a date based on our social security number, or state, or birthdate, or last name in the alphabet?

If you look hard enough, you will see that batching can, and does, occur somewhere at every level within every company. You just need to know what to look for!

Many companies batch all their evaluations in December. As a result, the managers never have enough time to do the evaluations correctly. So employees don't receive the proper feedback needed to improve, and the company ends up lacking in people development, bench-strength, and succession planning. Think of all the hidden costs that underlie this system.

When I worked for Honeywell, they did all their evaluations based on their employees' hiring date. This had the effect of level loading their evaluation process, so the managers did them naturally as one-piece flow. Now, managers and

---

* Personal conversation with Lauren Protzman on 4 April 2015—used with
  permission.

employees have time to complete their evaluations, complete their 360° feedback, and discuss their employees' career paths and development plans. Employee morale is better, the company develops their people and people have a "feel" for their future. Which company would you rather work for?

We all batch—it is human nature. It's something we do naturally and we don't think about it. After learning about batching and its consequences, you find it easier to point out to others. The ironic part is nobody wants to be told they are batching. I liken it to the knowledge we have now about smoking. It's like if you came to me asking for health advice, while slugging your way through an entire pack of cigarettes, and I *don't* tell you how dangerous they are for you. While this example is a bit extreme in comparison, the principles are the same. People are offended when you tell them they batch. They will fight you on it and try to prove to you how batching is better and faster. More times than not, they are fighting you over something they "believe in," but 5 minutes prior to this, they didn't consciously even know they were doing it.

The CrossFit Story*

I am an avid CrossFitter and experienced a batching scenario at the gym the other day. I was training for a competition, and we were practicing for one of the three workouts. The workout requires 10 stations and 1 minute of weight-lifting at each station. At each one of these stations is a barbell with a prescribed amount of weight, in increasing increments of 10 lb. at each station (135, 145, 155, 165, etc.). I was with two other guys and we all said, "Okay let's go ahead and set it up." I instantly thought about the batching vs. the one-piece flow way to do it.

---

* Story from Dan Protzman, http://www.crossfit.com/.

There are two racks of barbells on the wall to the right of the room, a stack of weights to the right of the barbells, and the open end of the room we were going to use was to the far left side of the gym. The other two guys immediately started removing all 10 barbells from the wall and carrying them over to the left side of the room. I immediately stopped them and asked what they were doing. They informed me they were setting up and were confused as to why I stopped them. I suggested a different approach: "Why don't you grab one barbell off the wall, carry it 10 ft to the weight plate stack, load the bar, and roll the barbell to the space it needs to be?" They looked at me like I had five heads and said, "What's the difference?"

I explained to them that by moving all of the bars first, you are now going to have to pick up and carry all of the weight plates over to the barbells. This is going to require much more effort and energy. They also have now allowed room for error, because they need to keep track of which station has the correct amount of weight on it. They could easily have three barbells with the same weight (155, 155, 155), instead of the incremented weight difference (135, 145, 155). I then showed them that by loading each barbell immediately, it required less storage space, and we could all work together in a short work-cell, and if one finished we could "bump" down to the next person to do the step they were working on, which would be secure with a weight clip and roll the weight to the intended location.

The two guys stared at me dumbfounded after I explained this to them, and, while a bit skeptical and unsure, we did things the way I suggested. Once we were finished, one of the guys looked at me and said, "I don't think that made a difference at all." I knew he was confused but told him, "The sad thing is, you wouldn't notice the difference until you did it both ways and saw the errors and opportunities for defects doing it the batch way."

At this point I had their interest but not their understanding. I instructed them to put all the weight back and try it again. We tried the original batch method with some people who had just arrived, and sure enough, the other athletes were winded, tired, and had messed up the order in two different locations, as well as having 2 barbells with the same amount of weight (165 and 165). The amount of time they spent trying to find which barbell was missing struck home to my two guys. They looked at me and said, "Wow, I get it, who would have thought that something so simple could make such a big difference."

Batching is batching; it doesn't matter if it is in a gym, manufacturing plant, bank, government office, corporate office, or even putting away your groceries. We all do it, and we can all help those that do it … you just need to understand they're doing it. That's why we wrote this book.

This innate—call it primal—need we have to batch hasn't developed and evolved as the rest of human nature has. We are not being chased by wild animals and forced to grab handfuls of berries and meat at a time. We are civilized and produce things efficiently. It is time we change our primal function from batch to flow!

Chapter 4

I'm Going to Need a Few More Examples

One-piece flow isn't the easiest of concepts to understand. After all, if it were easy to understand and perceived as correct, we wouldn't all have the issues we currently have today. Here are some more examples that cover many different sectors. My experience is that for many people, it takes hearing *that one example* that really "brings it home" in order for it to click. So, with that in mind, please enjoy the following.

Have you ever had contractors perform work in your house? It could be electricians, plumbers, etc. They all batch their work. The electricians will put in all the electrical boxes, then wire them all, then put in the outlets (plugs), then install the covers. During this process, you will see them making multiple trips to their trucks and sometimes to the nearest home improvement store because they don't make sure they have everything they need prior to starting the job. This wastes tons of time, and you, the homeowner, have to pay for their inefficiency.

In construction, if builders are working on multiple properties at a time, they will pour the cement for each house or building, then do the framing for each one, then do the

HVAC,* then the plumbing, etc. No one can move in until the first house, or building, has all the construction completed.

Landscapers batch by sending all their trucks first thing in the morning, at the same time, to get mulch, and then they find all their trucks waiting in line behind each other (queue) and losing significant time. What if they staggered their start times for each truck and schedules for the day so when their trucks arrived they wouldn't have to wait in line?

Doctors make rounds to see their patients. How do they round? They grab a bunch of charts and then go to see the patients. The first patient's orders don't get to the unit clerk until the last patient is seen. This is changing in some cases with electronic order entry, but only if the doctors enter each patient's orders immediately after seeing each patient.

Surgeons start off the morning with 7:30 a.m. case starts (batching). This means the hospital has to have all their operating rooms (ORs) and patients ready to go at 7:30 a.m. Then the parade to the ORs begins. While the doctors are operating in parallel, think about what this does to the hospital and the patients! The patients have to arrive by 5:30 a.m. or earlier. The hospital has to have its largest staffing of the day ready in order to handle this large demand of patients. It starts with registration, pre-op care, surgery (OR), post-op recovery room (PAC-U), and, for some, rooms on the hospital floors (units). It creates constant chaos with the surgeons, who are regularly angry and upset when they discover their patient isn't ready. This leads to a phenomenon whereby the surgeons then tell their first three or four patients to arrive at 5:30 a.m. or sooner, so if one of them is not ready, maybe another will be. This further magnifies the problem. Now the pre-op area is out of beds and has to use PAC-U beds to house all these patients. Surgeons in many cases are their own worst enemies but don't realize it! However, we are all like the surgeons. None of us is immune to this batch thinking mindset.

---

* HVAC = typical acronym for heating, ventilating, air conditioning.

My daughter-in-law Lauren* states, "After we talked the other day, we stopped for snowballs at a snowball stand. I was behind someone who ordered 6 snowballs of different sizes and 3 different flavors. Now that my eyes were opened to batching, I was so frustrated because it took us forever to get our snowballs. First she, the snowball person, put out each of the six cups. Then she took out each flavor and set it on the counter. Then she double-checked with each person in the family to make sure what they wanted. Then she put the first layer of ice in each cup. Then she added some flavor to each one (two at a time). Then she added more ice and then some more flavor to each one. If she had just done one-piece flow she would not have had to remove the flavors or double-checked with each person or picked up and put down each cup several times as she batched the order." Lauren also mentioned that if the worker had prepared the snowballs with one-piece flow, she would have been able to enjoy her snowball a lot faster!

At dinner one evening, Lauren proceeded to update me on her grading papers example we discussed earlier in the book. It took her husband to prod her a bit, but she hesitantly told me that she tried grading papers one-piece flow and she got done before all the other teachers. She didn't like it because it was so uncomfortable but couldn't believe it worked. All her fellow teachers couldn't believe it either. Are they converts? Probably not yet, but they now know, regardless of which they choose, which one is more efficient.

In a hospital, the nutritional services department is preparing sandwiches[†] (see Figure 4.1). The cook goes to get a large rack of trays. She takes out all the trays and places them across several tables. She gets as many loaves of bread as she can carry from the pantry room and then bags of turkey from the fridge. First she opens up each loaf of bread. Then she takes

---

* Personal conversation with Lauren Protzman, 4/5/2015.
† Example is from *Leveraging Lean in Ancillary Hospital Services: Creating a Cost Effective, Standardized, High Quality, Patient-Focused Operation*, Charles Protzman, Joyce Kerpchar, George Mayzell, MD, MBA, FACP © 2014 CRC Press.

Figure 4.1   Batching sandwiches. (From BIG Archives.)

the bread and puts each piece down, side by side, on each tray until she has every tray full with one layer of bread. Next she opens up all the bags of sliced turkey. Next comes one slice of turkey on each piece of bread. Then she grabs two pieces of bread together and places them on top of the turkey for each sandwich. This was actually a process improvement they implemented before we started working with them. Next, another slice of turkey is placed on each one, and finally the last piece of bread. Now our first sandwich is complete.

But how long have they been sitting out so far? Would you believe about 45 minutes? But we are not done yet. Now she takes each sandwich and cuts it diagonally in half. This takes another 10 minutes. She places each stack into a plastic holder. And finally she puts all the trays back on the rack to transport to the plastic sealing machine. Now, after more than 60 minutes, we have our first sandwich wrapped in plastic. It is sold as a "fresh" sandwich, but, at this point, would you call it fresh?

But wait; we are not done yet. Once they are all sealed she puts them back in the rack and then moves the rack back to the working table where she started. She takes out each tray and puts on the sticker with the "freshness" date and price.

Finally they go back into the refrigerator to be pulled out as needed for the front counter.

What problems does this system create? Yes, I said system. Batching is a system, and with it come all the problems of batching.

First, the bread and turkey are exposed to the "environment" for over an hour prior to being wrapped. The bread starts to dry out and get "crusty." Next, we find if they don't sell all the sandwiches, some have to be thrown out. For some of their other sandwiches, like chicken salad, or tuna, the bread turns real soggy by the time the patient's family opens it up.

How would a flow process have worked? In this case, we don't make the sandwich until it is ordered. This is a completely different system! Then we have all our lettuce, meats, etc. laid out in the proper order, in a refrigerated sandwich prep table, like Subway has, and make the sandwiches one-piece flow to the consumer's expectation. Which sandwich would you rather have (see Figure 4.2)? Everything in our flow world/system is focused around the customer first, giving

Baseline metrics salad			Baseline metrics sandwich	
Operators	2		Operators	6
Units per day	300		Units per day	1,050
Units per operator	150		Units per operator	175
Space	300 sq. ft		Space	448 sq. ft

Lean metrics salad and sandwich combined		
Operators	3	−62.5%
Units per day	1,639	+17%
Units per operator	546	+69%
Space	375 sq. ft	−50%

No one was laid off, but some team members were cross-trained and moved to other areas.

Figure 4.2   Salad/sandwich line results. 1/26/2005. (From BIG Archives.)

them what they want. Then we focus on how we make the employee's job as easy as possible.

Believe it or not, batching occurs every Christmas/holiday season. And who is guilty? Most of you reading this book! How many of you batch your holiday cards? Most of you will fill in all the cards or write notes or letters. Then you will stuff all the cards into envelopes, and finally you will address them and then put on the stamps. It's amazing how, even in some of the smallest tasks we perform, batching finds a way to work its way in.

Companies even batch their accounts payable. How often have you been told you have to wait for the next "check run" in order to be paid? Batching occurs in the printing/publishing industry all the time. This book was batched all the way through the process. Instead of processing it chapter by chapter, the entire book is submitted, all the editing is completed, the reviews are done in batch, and finally the book is printed in batches. Chapter by chapter would go much quicker. However, how could one incorporate "one-book flow"? Some books now are self-published. In this case the books are printed as orders are received vs. printing them in advance. Now there is software available that can publish every draft of a book simultaneously, showing the true beauty of the creative process.*

We find batching even occurs in many "one-piece flow" or highly touted Lean lines. I can't tell you how many "world-class" factories, offices, or warehouses I visit that still batch, and the scary part is they *think* they are doing one-piece flow.

Batching is evident in factories whenever you see

■ WIP (work in process) or kanban squares between process steps (see Figure 4.3)., or

---

* Software that can publish every draft of a book simultaneously shows the true beauty of the creative process, http://qz.com/335942/an-author-used-a-tool-for-programmers-to-write-a-book/, http://qz.com/author/mmurphyqz/, supplied by Steve and Julie Stenberg via email correspondence, dated 1/31/2015.

Figure 4.3   Work in process in between stations. (From BIG Archives.)

- Operators* surrounded by partially assembled product (WIP).

Batching also occurs whenever workers "build ahead." This could be because the next person in line is still working, someone called in sick, there are part shortages for the next assembly, or simply because they are idle and "they can!" The unfortunate part is they think they are saving time when, in fact, they're creating more of a gap between them and the next person ahead. What they are doing is creating more inventory which is costing us money.

Beware! Batching is all around us, every day, and it kills our productivity!

---

* The authors use the term operators to refer to anyone doing the work, whether they are team members, workers, office staff, nurses, doctors, etc.

Chapter 5

Let's Get into This a Little Deeper, Shall We?

A Very Detailed Comparison of Batching to One-Piece Flow

So let's explore what batching is in more detail. Listed below is a simple example of batching the assembly of an ink pen:

Let's assemble 500 pens. Figure 5.1 shows how parts are typically delivered to the floor, work center, or even office areas. Normally they are delivered on a pallet or are stored on a shelf, but often the parts get mixed up and are presented as a mess. Many times the parts are short, i.e., missing completely or the counts are off, some parts are broken, rusty, or have other quality issues.

This pen has five parts, and we have all the parts we need; in fact we even have some extra parts, just in case (see Figure 5.2).

1. Housing
2. Ink pen
3. Spring
4. Tip
5. Rubber piece

Figure 5.1   Batch of pen parts. (From BIG Archives.)

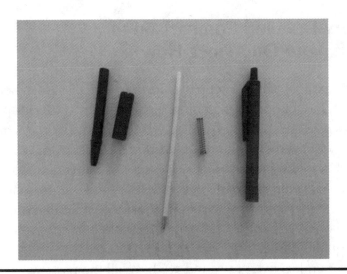

Figure 5.2   Individual pen parts. (From BIG Archives.)

The pen must be assembled in a particular order, and there are some key points to its assembly. Step 1 is to assemble the spring and the ink pen (see Figure 5.3).

Step 2 is to assemble the spring and ink pen assembly into the housing (see Figure 5.4).

Figure 5.3   Spring onto ink pen assembly. (From BIG Archives.)

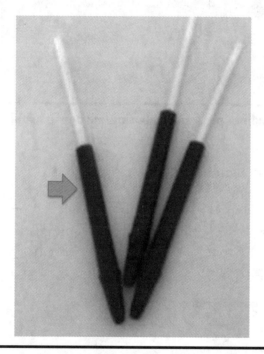

Figure 5.4   Ink pen assembly into housing assembly. (From BIG Archives.)

Step 3 is to assemble the rubber piece onto the housing (see Figure 5.5), and Step 4 is to push on the clip part of the housing (see Figure 5.6).

So if you had to assemble 100 of these pens, how would *you* do it?

Most of us, 99.9%, would assemble all 100 of the ink pens and springs first. Then, we would put all of the assemblies into the housings. Then, we would put the rubber piece on

Figure 5.5 Rubber piece onto housing/ink pen assembly. (From BIG Archives.)

each one, and then assemble the tip. This process of assembly is called batching.

"So what," you say? What is wrong with assembling them in a batch process? Well to start off, batching is very inefficient. "How can that be" you ask? Well, let's analyze the above example step by step.

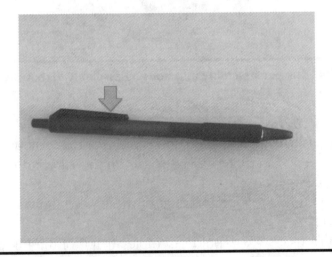

Figure 5.6 Push on the clip part of the housing—now it is a completed pen assembly. (From BIG Archives.)

First we assemble 100 springs to 100 ink pens. Normally these springs will be in some type of bag and the ink pens in some type of box. So the steps for this are:

1. Pick up the ink pen and hold it in one of your hands. 1 second.
2. Pick up the spring and hold it in your other hand. 1 second.
3. Assemble the spring to the ink pen. 1 second.
4. Set the assembly down. 1 second.
5. Do this for the next 99 pieces. 99×4 seconds$=396$ seconds.

Now I have 100 ink pens and assemblies (see Figure 5.7) and a total time of 400 seconds and 400 steps. How much space do we need? Well, we need enough space to hold 100 of these ink pen assemblies at this point. In manufacturing terms this is considered work in process (WIP) inventory. Inventory costs money, and so does space. In addition, most companies need to have computer systems to keep track of all this inventory. They also have finance departments, which have to make sure it is all there, accounted for, and still good product, which

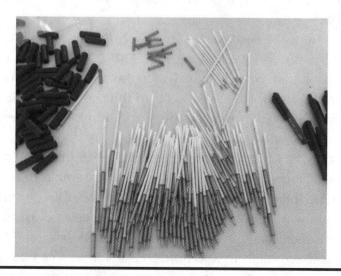

Figure 5.7 We have assembled 100 ink pens and springs. We had to keep counting along the way until we got to 100. Notice some were left over. (From BIG Archives.)

is yet another cost. If it takes 1 second for each step, I now have expended a minimum of 4 seconds of total labor time for each piece.

Now I have this pile of ink pens and springs; what is the next step?

6. Pick up the ink pen and spring assembly carefully with one hand. Note: The problem now is I have this huge pile of parts. If you are not careful, the spring can slip off the ink pen, which is what happened to me. So I had to pick up the spring again and assemble it onto the ink pen. 1 second.
7. Pick up the housing with the other hand. 1 second.
8. Put it into the housing. 1 second.
9. Set the housing and ink pen assembly down on the table. 1 second.
10. Do this for the next 99 pieces. 99×4 seconds = 396 seconds.

Note: I need additional space on the table because I don't want to mix up the ink pen assemblies with the housing assemblies.

Let's count the seconds so far. If we don't include the rework I had to do we add another 400 seconds to the previous total of 400 seconds, which now gives us 800 seconds and another 400 steps. However, keep in mind the rework is real and occurs in every manufacturing and administrative environment. Let's move on.

We now have 100 housings, partially assembled (more WIP) (see Figure 5.8). The next step is to assemble the rubber piece. One must be careful because the rubber piece can only go on one way. If not trained properly it is easy to assemble this piece incorrectly, which will cause additional time when the tip is assembled. In addition, the pen assembly can easily slide out of the housing assembly when you pick it up. In fact, looking at the table in front of me I can see some have already started falling out!

Figure 5.8   Assembling the ink pens into the housings. (From BIG Archives.)

The next step is

11. Pick up the housing assembly. 1 second.
12. Pick up the rubber piece. 1 second.
13. Slide the rubber piece onto the housing (this takes an extra 2 seconds of time). 3 seconds.
14. Put the housing assembly back down on the table. 1 second.
15. Assemble the balance of 99 pieces. 6 seconds × 99 = 594 seconds.

Add 600 seconds to our 800 seconds for a total of 1,400 seconds and another 400 steps. Again, this assumes we had no trouble picking up the housings without the pen assemblies falling out. We also now need more space and an inventory location for the housing and rubber piece assemblies*. More WIP and more space! Just a quick mental check

---

* Some companies will even take these assemblies and put them in stock so they can pick them again for the work order for the next step. Think of how much waste this creates.

for all of us—we have completed 1,200 steps, and have we written anything yet with a completed pen? No. Have we sold a completed pen yet and turned inventory into a receivable or, better yet, cash? No. Ok, just checking, let's move on.

The next step:

16. Pick up the housing assembly. Once again I must be careful of the pen and ink assembly falling out of the housing assembly, and I have some rework ahead of me looking at this pile of pens on the table. 1 second.
17. Pick up the tip with the other hand. 1 second.
18. Screw on the tip to the housing assembly. 2 seconds.
19. Put the assembly back down on the table. 1 second.
20. Assemble the balance of 99 pieces.

This step takes 5 seconds to assemble, and if we are the first pen, we then wait for 495 seconds as we assemble the other 99 pieces. Again, this is not counting any rework or problems. We add this 500 seconds to our prior 1,400, and we end up with 1,900 seconds and another 400 steps. However, we now need another inventory location, more space, and WIP!

The next step is to put the pens in the box (see Figure 5.9). Each box holds five pens. So we now look down at our pile of pens, and do we grab one pen at a time? Of course not, we grab a bunch of pens and then stuff the pens into the box, side by side. The steps are:

21. Pick up a bunch of pens (it is a different number of pens every time) with one hand. But let's say we don't have any problems and grab exactly the right amount of pens each time, even though we know sometimes we will get two or three pens and other times four to six pens, and then we have to orient them properly or orient them as we pick them up. 2 seconds.
22. Pick up the box. 1 second.
23. Load each pen in the box. 3 seconds.

Figure 5.9   Put pens in box. (From BIG Archives.)

24. Close the box with two hands. But this means I have to set any extra pens in my hand down on the table first! And then grab the lid with the free hand and close the box. 2 seconds.
25. Put the box down. 1 second.
26. Repeat this process for 19 more boxes. 19×9 second= 171 s.

Now we are 1,900 seconds+180 or 2,080 seconds and another 100 steps. Again we have more WIP, more space, and another inventory location.

The last step is to pack the small boxes into the larger box. The steps are:

27. Pick up a bunch of boxes. Again, quantity will vary. 3 seconds.
28. Place them in the larger box. Chances are, for this step we are going to have to use our hands at some point to organize the box. 2 seconds.
29. Repeat the process four times. 4×5 seconds=20 seconds.
30. Close and seal the box. 5 seconds.

This gives us a subtotal of 25 seconds and a minimum of 9 steps.

We now have a grand total of 2,105 seconds and 1,709 steps in this process (assuming we don't count any rework). We have a total of 33 seconds of actual process time with the balance being storage. (Note the 33 seconds includes the time to pack the pens in the boxes. It does not amortize the box time per pen.) We call this WIP stored labor capacity. This is because we have added labor to the WIP, but it is now stuck in the process until it is completed. We have an average cycle time (CT) of 21.05 seconds per piece. But this is misleading, because even though the first piece is completed and boxed at 2,085 seconds, we don't really see it until the entire lot is completed. So our real cycle time for the batch is 2,105 seconds, which is the same as the throughput time.

Once again, for this final step we need more space to package up the pens and to store the completed boxes, which requires more space, more WIP, and another possible inventory location. We would normally only assign an inventory location if we were to stock the WIP created at any of the process steps back into the stockroom, to be pulled out later or assign a finished goods location. One can imagine what the WIP would look like if a bunch of loose housing assemblies at any point in the process were transported to the stockroom, put away, picked, and then sent back out to the floor. This is a real-life scenario and still occurs at many production plants today, all over the world. The stocking of subassemblies is not as uncommon as one might think.

So, What Problems Are Created by Our Batching Example Listed Above?

Can a product get damaged in storage or while it is being transported? We see it every day! (see Figures 5.10 and 5.11).

Figure 5.10   Parts potentially damaged during transport. (From BIG Archives.)

Figure 5.11   Parts damage occurs in storage. (From BIG Archives.)

Figure 5.12   This car was hidden in the junk storage area for years!

Like in the picture, whenever we pile things up in an area, closet, attic, etc., things get partially damaged or permanently broken or sometimes lost. At one company, they were cleaning up an area and found a car! (see Figure 5.12). The company made automotive mirrors and somewhere along the way had misplaced this car.* We also have the real possibility of quite a bit of rework in this simple process. Many times the parts are not counted out correctly, so we have to stop at some or even several points to figure out how many we have assembled. In the process above there are 1,709 such opportunities for defects to occur!

Principle: Each Step in the Process Is an Opportunity for a Defect to Occur

Cycle Time and Throughput Time

Cycle time is equal to

1. The time each piece comes off the line

---

* *Mapping Your Value Stream*, Donnelly Mirrors, SME video, http://www.multime-diahrd.com/catpdf/SME%20Catalog.pdf.

2. The total time it takes to complete one piece divided by the number of operators
3. The amount of work each operator has—in reality, the slowest operator or machine (if it is slower than the operator cycle time), or
4. In the batch environment, the total processing time from start to finish divided by the total number of pieces produced

When one batches, it is virtually impossible to calculate the real cycle time because there is so much waste in the process. Many times people try to compare batch to one-piece flow by just timing the individual steps, but again this doesn't take into account all the extra waste in the batch system. The only way to try to calculate cycle time in a batch environment is to take the total time for a lot of parts or some number of pieces or paperwork and divide it by the total number of pieces produced in the lot. However, this doesn't represent true cycle time, because they are completed not one at a time but in a batch at the end of the process.

Authors' Note: *If you want to be fair, you cannot compare the cycle time of batch to flow by just taking the times for each step, i.e., time study, for each operator. Batching includes so much more waste that can only be captured by taking the time for the entire process for a batch or lot of parts, whereas one-piece flow can be figured out by one of the first three methods above.*

We have found most batch-based factories (or offices) keep no records for cycle time or throughput time. Most of the time, the output is what someone "remembers" it to be, which is normally the highest number ever assembled or completed in an hour or a day. It doesn't take into account that zero may have been completed the day before.

Throughput time is the total time it takes to get something through the process from raw material (RM to finished goods (FG).

(a)

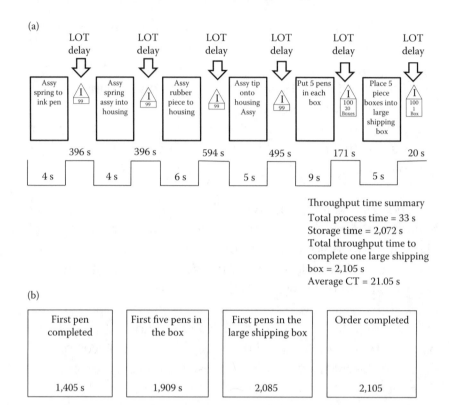

Throughput time summary
Total process time = 33 s
Storage time = 2,072 s
Total throughput time to
complete one large shipping
box = 2,105 s
Average CT = 21.05 s

(b)

First pen completed	First five pens in the box	First pens in the large shipping box	Order completed
1,405 s	1,909 s	2,085	2,105

We don't see the first pen until the batch is completed, which in this case is 2,105 s, however our first pen is completed at 1,405 s, in the first small box at 1,909 s, and in the large box at 2,085 s. This means if our customer really needs these pens right away, we can't get him the first box of five until 1,909 s.

Figure 5.13   (a) Pen value stream map. (b) Pen CT stats. (From BIG Archives.)

This is what a value stream map (VSM)* will show you once the timeline is completed (see Figure 5.13a). In the VSM, each box is a step in the process, and each triangle represents storage (WIP) in between each process. A batching delay is

---

* The value stream map is a tool used to map the process from the beginning to the end. An example used in the book *Lean Thinking* by Womack and Jones looks at a can of soda from the bauxite mine (where the aluminum is mined) to the consumer, which took over 300 days. The VSM is defined in *Learning to See: Value Stream Mapping to Add Value and Eliminate MUDA*, Mike Rother and John Shook, foreword Jim Womack, foreword Dan Jones © 1999 Lean Enterprise Institute.

called a *lot delay* because the entire lot is waiting for the next step in the process. *One only finds lot delays where batching is occurring.*

Some companies refer to "throughput time" as "cycle time"; however, it is important to differentiate the two. Remember, our definition of throughput time is from the beginning of the lot until the first one is completed and in the shipping box. In the pen assembly example above it is 2,105 seconds. If we divide this by 100 pieces we have a rough approximation of the cycle time: that is 21.05 seconds per piece. In reality, it will be more than this because there will be problems picking these parts up, doing rework etc. Also, it should be noted we are just looking at the in-process cycle times. We are not counting the storage time for raw material or finished goods.

If we had six operators, one at each step, or each operator assembling their own complete batch, our cycle time would be equal to the slowest operator. In this case it would be operator #5 with 9 seconds of work every fifth cycle. (This assumes no rework or movement of parts from station to station.) In reality with six operators, operator #5 would be putting the pens away as they came to him (one-piece flow) because he would not want to be idle. This would be the same case with operator #6. This would make the cycle time 6 seconds, which is the bottleneck process, at station #3.

When Do We Get Our First Pen?

We don't see the first pen until the batch is completed, which in this case is 2,105 seconds. Our first pen is completed at 1,405 seconds in the first small box at 1,909 seconds and in the large box at 2,085 seconds. This means if our customer really needs these pens right away, we can't get him the first box of five until 1,909 seconds (see Figure 5.13b). It also means we delay our liquidity improvement from inventory to receivable or to cash for the same length of time.

Let's say you work for the government or a not-for-profit organization, and liquidity (cash flow) is not terribly relevant to you, but time is of the essence. Think about how long it takes to provide services to your constituents with a process built on batching throughout the supply chain delivery system. But everyone wins by reducing the throughput time ... everyone, and this can only be accomplished by shifting to a new paradigm/process based on flow.

Space

How much space do we need for the above example? We need space before the first operation (to put WIP as it arrives), the last location (to put WIP or FG after it is completed), and in between each of the six major operations (to put WIP). If we had six operators assembling, we would need approximately 4 ft (1.2 meters) of space per operator or 24 square feet (2.2 square meters) of space. This would be equal to three or four tables. This space, even when empty, is tied up because it is reserved for the entire inventory.

WIP

In our batch system, with one operator, we would always have 100 pieces of WIP in lot delay after each operation until the final two steps, where it would reduce to 20 pieces (boxes) and then one piece (box). If we had six operators assembling we would have up to 600 pieces or more WIP in the system.

Does this really seem like an efficient system to you? Most of you will now try to find flaws in my logic, or my times etc., and come back with some type of argument as to why I am wrong and that my assumptions are not correct.* Some

---

* Please feel free to email me at danprotzman@biglean.com or charlieprotzman@ biglean.com.

of you will even go out of your way to convince me that this approach is indeed the most efficient and will fight to keep your ability to batch at any cost.

Don't believe me? Ask any person who tries to implement one-piece flow. They will all agree. Everyone will fight to keep his or her current ability to batch at almost any cost, no matter how many examples we show them on paper; or simulations we run with pens, flashlights, Lego bricks; or pilots (experiments)* we run in the factory. What you will typically hear is that flow stuff might work on "that line" but it won't work on ours … we're unique.

What Is Flow?

Flow is the smooth, uninterrupted movement of a product or information construct from beginning to end. To truly flow means once you start to work on something, you don't stop until the task is completed. It can be one person, many people, or machines doing the task, but there are no stops along the way.

Let's look at a traffic example. Have you ever been on a major city street (thoroughfare) and had to stop at every single @#%&% red light? Do you ever say to yourself, why don't they time these lights (to the speed limit) so I can just flow smoothly to my destination? This is the same concept, just on an all-encompassing scale.

There are four things necessary to sustain flow:

1. Transport
2. Inspect
3. Process
4. Storage

---

* Experiments is the term used in place of pilots by Guy Parsons in his book *Out of the Question: How Curious Leaders Win Paperback,* Guy Parsons, Allan Milham © 2014 Advantage Media.

When something is inspected or stored, it interrupts the flow. When people batch, it also interrupts the flow. Toll booths are another example of a place where you have to stop and are stored until you pay a toll. EZ Pass or SunPass allow you to continue to flow.

How Does Batch Compare to One-Piece Flow?

One-piece flow should always be the goal. Many will compromise on this goal if necessary, in order to obtain some improvement, but ultimately, any compromise still results in waste; it just might be *less* waste than before.

Let's walk through the pen assembly example with one-piece flow:

1. Pick up the ink pen and hold it in your hand. 1 second.
2. Pick up the spring and hold it in your other hand. 1 second.
3. Assemble the spring to the ink pen. 1 second.
4. Pick up the housing with the other hand. 1 second.
5. Put it into the housing with two hands. 1 second.
6. Pick up the rubber piece with one hand. 1 second.
7. Slide the rubber piece onto the housing in the other hand. 3 seconds.
8. Pick up the tip with the free hand. 1 second.
9. Screw on the tip to the housing assembly with both hands. 2 seconds.
10. Pick up the small box. 1 second.
11. Load the pen in the small box. 1 second.
12. Put the box down. 1 second.

Total 15 seconds and 12 steps per pen, or 1,200 steps and 1,500 seconds for 100 pens.

13. Every fifth unit. Close the box with two hands. 2 seconds × 20 boxes = 40 seconds and 20 steps.

14. Every fifth unit. Place them in the larger box. 2 seconds×
    20 boxes=40 seconds and 20 steps.
15. Close and seal the box. 5 seconds and 1 step.

Total 85 seconds and 41 steps. Grand total 1,585 seconds and 1,241 steps.

So, What Differences Do We See between Batching and One-Piece Flow?

In the process above there are 1,241 steps compared to 1,709 steps in batch. This is a reduction of 27% of the steps and opportunities for defects!

Principle: Each Step in the Process Is an Opportunity for a Defect to Occur

Cycle Time and Throughput Time

Our total process time is now 19 seconds. Throughput time is 79 seconds in order to get one box of pens into the final shipping box. This means if a customer really needed a box of five pens right away we could have them ready in 75 seconds, assuming we don't spend 4 seconds to put them in the final shipping box. If they needed just one pen, we now have the flexibility to supply it in just 12 seconds (with no packaging). Notice that we still have some lot delays at the end of the process, caused by the boxing of the pens. Therefore we still have to assemble all the pens before they can be shipped. With our lot delays this equals 1,585 seconds compared to 2,105 seconds. This is a 25% reduction in throughput time. (see Figure 5.14).

Our cycle time is still a little difficult to calculate because we are, in fact, batching when we put them in the smaller and larger boxes.

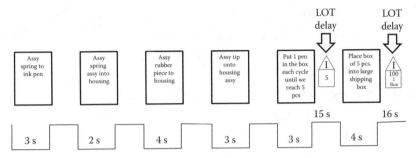

Throughput time summary
- Total process time = 19 s
- Storage time = 31 s
- Average CT = 12 s (prior to box) and 15.8 overall
- Time to first pen in 5 piece box = 15 s and first 5 in large box = 79 s
- Throughput time = 79 s for first box in shipping box. 1,585 s until last pen is in the shipping box. (1,200 + 300 first box + 85 final box is sealed)

Figure 5.14   Pen value stream map. (From BIG Archives.)

For the pen assembly, we average 12 seconds per pen—cycle time. Every fifth unit we have to add 2 seconds of cycle time to close the small box and 2 seconds of cycle time to put them in the larger box (total 4 seconds—every five pieces), with the last cycle adding an additional 5 seconds to close the large box every 100 pieces.

If we divide 1,585 seconds by 100 pieces we have a rough approximation of the cycle time, which is 15.85 seconds per piece compared to over 21.05 seconds for batching.

Station-Balanced Line

If this were a station-balanced line,* where each of the six operators worked at an assembly station, then the cycle time

---

* A station-balanced line is where each station is time studied, normally by a process or manufacturing engineer, to have the same amount of time allocated at each station for each operator. Operators are almost always sitting down. However, once the line is set up it is very difficult to maintain balance as operators change or improvements are made. If an operator is out sick then the other operators struggle to get all the parts out. Because of normal variation in the operators' times, WIP caps—kanbans—are installed in between the operators, where the operators are supposed to stop assembly once the cap, or limit, is reached.

would equal 4 seconds per piece/box (assembly of the rubber piece is our constraint). Operator #6 would have a lot of idle time as he has to wait while operator #5 puts five pieces in a box before he, #6, can do any work. On the final piece, the cycle time would increase to 5 seconds since operator #6 has to seal the box (1 second).

When Do We Get Our First Pen?

With one-piece flow, our first pen is completed in the amazing time of 12 seconds, and we have five in the first small box at 77 seconds vs. 1,909 seconds, which is a 95.9% reduction in initial throughput time and is very normal for one-piece flow implementations (see Figure 5.15).

Fact: With one-piece flow you will always get your first piece faster than batching!

Space

How much space do we need for the above example? We only need one station for all six major steps. We need space for

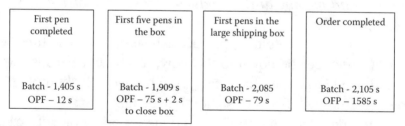

First pen completed	First five pens in the box	First pens in the large shipping box	Order completed
Batch - 1,405 s OPF – 12 s	Batch - 1,909 s OPF – 75 s + 2 s to close box	Batch - 2,085 OPF – 79 s	Batch - 2,105 s OFP – 1585 s

Batch throughput time summary

Total process time = 33 s
Storage time = 2,072 s
Total throughput time to complete one large shipping box = 2,105 s
Average CT = 21.05 s

OPF throughput time summary

- Total process time = 19 s
- Storage time = 31 s
- Average CT = 12 s (prior to box) and 15.8 overall
- Time to first pen in 5 piece box = 15 s and first 5 in large box = 79 s
- Throughput time = 79 s for first box in shipping box. 1,585 s until last pen is in the shipping box. (1,200 + 300 first box + 85 final box)

Figure 5.15   Pen CT stats. (From BIG Archives.)

parts bins on the table placed in the order they are assembled. We don't need any space in between each operation, like in batch, because we are making each piece one at a time from start to finish.

This means we need less than one table, which results in a 75% reduction in space with one operator compared to the original space required when batching. Again, this is a typical result.

WIP

If batching, one operator would always have 100 pieces of WIP until the final two steps, where it would reduce to 20 and then one. If we had six operators assembling we would have up to 600 pieces or more WIP in the system.

Authors' Note: *This is just a simple pen example, but it happens in real life every day. We find ourselves spending most of our time doing non-value-added activities like storing, moving, counting, and throwing out obsolete inventory. Wouldn't it be better if we could convert these to value-adding activities, which would eliminate obsolete inventory, counting, storing, and moving and increase our cash and job security (see Table 5.1)?*

If we had six operators, one at each step, our cycle time would no longer be equal to the slowest operator because we would use baton zone balancing, or what we call "bumping," to overcome the effects of station balancing.

Bumping starts with the last, and fastest operator. Let's call them operator #3. When they have completed their pen and put it in the box, they will bump back to the operator before them, in this case operator #2, and take the pen at whatever point it is assembled and continue to assemble it. Operator #2 will bump back to operator #1 and again take the pen at whatever point operator #1 is at and continue to produce it. Then operator #1 will go back to the very beginning and start

Table 5.1 Comparison of Batch to Flow

Aspect	Batch	Flow
Time for first completed piece	Longer—doesn't get completed until the last operation	Shortest—gets completed right away
WIP	Significant amounts	Least amount
Space	Takes up significant amounts	Least
Throughput time	Longer	Shorter—normally 90% or more
Cycle time for each piece completed	Doesn't exist. Has to be calculated based on an average	Easy to calculate and normally 50% faster than batch
Travel distance	Long	Short
Units completed/ worked hour	Long	Normally 30% to 70% faster than batching
Defects	If one is bad they are normally all bad	Defects are caught right away
Machines	One person to one machine	One person to multiple machines

Source: Authors.

another pen. Each operator continues to build until they are "bumped."

Therefore, 12 seconds divided by six operators would result in a cycle time of 2 seconds with an increase of .11 seconds every fifth cycle and 0.03 seconds on every 100th piece. This would equate to an approximate average cycle time of 2.133 seconds* compared to 6 seconds in batching mode.

---

* ((12 s × 5 pcs) + (4 s × 1 pc)) ÷ (5 pcs) ÷ (6 operators) = 64 ÷ 5 = 12.8 s ÷ 6 operators = 2.133 – does not include closing the large box)

So Which System Is More Efficient?

Does batching really seem like an efficient system to you? Once again, most of you will now try *even harder* to find flaws in my logic, my times, etc. and come back with some type of argument as to why I am wrong and my assumptions are not correct.* Everyone we work with wants to keep his or her current ability to batch—at almost any cost.

This phenomenon is the single biggest reason most factories and offices still batch today. Even "one-piece flow" lines still have batching going on, if you look hard enough. This is why any type of flow-based implementation is so difficult to sustain and why it keeps guys like me (one-piece flow consultants) in business.

However, once you "get it," when you start to truly understand, you will begin to look at everything differently. You will see "**it**," i.e., batching, everywhere. You will see "it" when you go to restaurants and retail stores and even in what you do in your home and everyday life … when you pay bills, when you are cooking, when you are doing odd jobs around the house, it is there!.

For instance, you get the mail, you take it inside, and you open each envelope and put the empty ones in a pile for the recycle bin. Then you take the pile and put it in the recycle container. You then take the pile of remaining mail into the office. Now you have to sit down and go through each item again, sort it, and go online to pay your bills. With one-piece flow we would take each piece of mail, one at a time, and either dispose of it to the recycle container or open it, pay it online, and then either trash or file it away. Even in this case I learned early to submit each payment online as I go; otherwise, by the time you get them all loaded (batch) and hit submit, it tells you that you have timed out and have to start

---

* Please feel free to email me at danprotzman@biglean.com or charlieprotzman@biglean.com.

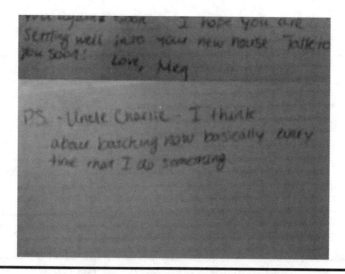

Figure 5.16   Note from my niece. (From note from Meg Protzman.)

over again. I'm sure I'm not the only person who's run into that error before?

My niece, a college junior at the time, was assisting her math professor with a research study at McDaniel College. During our conversation, I found out she was batching her process, so we ended up discussing, at some length, the principles and theory behind one-piece flow and how it applied to her research study project. A week or two later, she sent me a note* (see Figure 5.16) thanking me for meeting with her, and at the bottom she added: "P.S. Uncle Charlie—I think about batching now basically every time that I do something." I smiled to myself and thought, "Yes, she gets it."

Batching Model

In Figure 5.17, we show the difference between batching and flow. The top part of the model shows what happens

---

* Personal correspondence from Meg Protzman to Charlie Protzman, 7/18/2013.

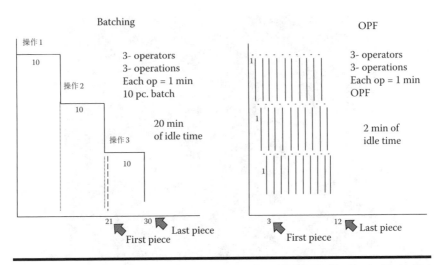

Figure 5.17   Batch vs. flow comparison. (From *The Effect of Lot Delay Reductions—Shigeo Shingo, The Shingo Production Management System,* © 1990 Productivity Press, p. 17, 116. Used with permission Taylor and Francis.)

with a 10-piece batch, three operators, and three operations, where each one takes 1 minute. It starts with operator #1. How long does it take operator #1 to complete a 10-piece batch if each one takes 1 minute? The answer is 10 minutes. Then we move to operator #2. How long does it take operator #2 to complete their operation? 10 minutes, and the same for operator #3, right? So when do we get our first piece? Most of you would say at 30 minutes, and you would be correct. We don't see the first piece until 30 minutes later. However, the first piece is actually completed at 21 minutes.

Now let's look at one-piece flow. How long does it take operator #1 to do one-piece? The answer is 1 minute. How long does it take operator #2 to do one-piece? 1 minute Operator #3? 1 minute. When do we get our first piece? 3 min. Note: This is compared to 21 minutes in the batch-designed environment described! When do we get our last piece? Before we answer this let's look back at the model.

Each operator is now doing one-piece flow so we will get a part every minute. This is called cycle time. Now when do we get the last piece? The answer is 12 minutes. Compared to 30 minutes in the batch scenario. Keep in mind that in this model we have not complicated it with all the batching waste and time that will be lost due to putting each piece down and picking it up again, or with defects not caught until the end of the process. This is why we contend that batching is the silent productivity killer!

Some of you will argue that this only happens on the first lot, and to some extent this is true; however, many companies dry their lines out each night* and start over the next day. In addition, as the work progresses, the batch system will continue to function more and more slowly compared to one-piece flow due to all the waste in the system.

A one-piece flow system converts all the idle time found in the batch process environment to productive (not necessarily value-added) time. The maximum idle time for the one-piece flow model is 3 minutes: 1 minute for operator #2 and two minutes for operator #3. In the batch example there are 30 minutes of idle time: 10 minutes for operator #2 and 20 minutes for operator #3. You might argue that the third operator would be doing something else until he gets his parts, and sometimes this is true, but many times we see them just sitting there idle.

How Do You Improve a Batch System?

In our pen exercise, can you think of ways we could improve upon the one-piece flow example? One way would be to

---

* To "dry out the line" means they complete all the WIP for that area or section. So the next day they have to build up the WIP again before they can complete the first piece. The opposite of this would be to leave the line "wet." This means all the WIP is left in place until the next day.

have the supplier ship all the small boxes already opened and vertically stored.* Then we could just load the pens in the box without having to pick up or put down the box. This eliminates steps 10 and 12 and saves 2 seconds. There are many more improvements we could make.

What Impact Does Size Have?

Most companies produce in large lots, sometimes 100 pieces, 500 pieces, or more. If we can't get them to do one-piece flow right away, we work to get them to at least try to reduce the lot size. If you reduce the lot size you can reduce the inventory and the space that goes with it.

The lot size defines the granularity of the inventory measure in the system. So if we cut the lot size by two then we simply have two lots in the system instead of one. There is no automatic inventory reduction; however, if we can now reduce the inventory, by one of the two lots, where we introduce only one smaller lot at a time, we can now work to reduce the inventory in the system. In a true "pull"† system, we can't start the next lot until the first lot has completed the first operation. In this system we cut the lot size all the way back through our supply chain. Toyota, for instance, works on 2 hours of inventory (not including safety stock).

---

* Suppliers can play a big role in helping you set up the one-piece flow environment. Many times the improvements made benefit the suppliers as well and help to lower your overall costs.
† A pull system is where the later process pulls from the earlier process. This is different than a batch or push type system where the parts are continually pushed from one operation to the next.

What Impact Does This Smaller Lot Size Have (See Figures 5.18 and 5.19)?

If we reduce the lot size we reduce the inventory in the system, and our cash goes up. If we reduce the inventory in the system our throughput time goes down (Little's Law), and we become more flexible supplying our customers. We find our mistakes quicker, thus improving quality and cutting scrap and defect costs.

Other Ideas?

Once we have one-piece flow, all our problems immediately come to the surface. This creates a ripe environment for ideas. For instance, what if we put a notch on the plastic ink pen, which would keep the spring from sliding off (see Figure 5.20)?

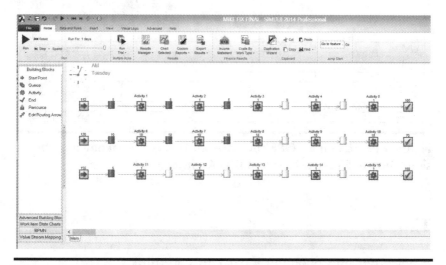

Figure 5.18 Simulation results batch vs. OPF comparison. The top line is a station balanced line with 5 pc WIP cap. The second line is a 10 pc batch. The third line is a one-piece flow line. (From BIG Archives.)

Given						
Five Operators	**Batch of 10 Pieces**					
Available Time = 450 min/ day						
Five Operations (Minutes)	2	1	4.5	4	3	
	A B C D E					
Cycle Time (ESTIMATE)					14.5	
Throughput Time					145	
Total Inventory in the system					40	
WIP between Ops					10	
First Piece					118	
Last Piece					145	
Quality if problem at A found at E					45	
Avg Pieces Possible Per Day	75 pieces possible (but you will only see 70 due to 10 pc batch)				70	

OPF Station Balanced

Five Operations (Minutes)	2	1	4.5	4	3	% to Batch
	A B C D E					
Cycle Time					4.5	69%
Throughput Time					14.5	90%
Total Invenentory in the system	With wip caps (5pcs prior to stations 2 & 3)				9.5	76%
WIP between Ops	Max With WIP Caps				5	50%
First Piece					14.5	88%
Last Piece					14.5	90%
Quality if problem at A found at E					4	91%
Total Pieces Per Day	If Line is Wet (If dry 96pcs is max)				100	43%

Bumping

Five Operations (Minutes)	2	1	4.5	4	3	% to OPF SB	% to Batch
	A B C D E						
Cycle Time					2.9	36%	80%
Throughput Time					2.9	80%	98%
Total Invenentory in the system					5	47%	88%
WIP between Ops					0	100%	100%
First Piece					2.9	80%	98%
Last Piece					2.9	80%	98%
Quality if problem at A found at E					4	0%	91%
Total Pieces Per Day					155	55%	122%

Figure 5.19 Batch vs. OPF comparison. This is a breakdown of the simulation in Figure 5.18 (From BIG Archives.)

Timeout 3

What other improvement ideas can you think of (see Timeout 3)?

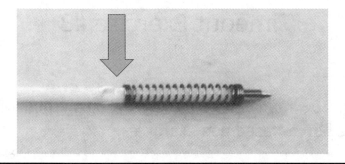

Figure 5.20   Notch in ink pen to clip in and position spring. (From BIG Archives.)

Timeout Exercise #3

- List how many improvements you can think of for the batch-based pen example.

_____
_____
_____
_____
_____
_____
_____
_____
_____
_____

- *Do you process your parts or paperwork this way? If so, list a few.*

_____
_____
_____
_____
_____
_____
_____
_____
_____
_____

- *Which process is really more efficient?*

_____
_____
_____
_____
_____
_____
_____
_____
_____

Chapter 6

The Eight Root Causes of Batching

How the Batch Process Occurs: Like It or Not, Sometimes We Have to Batch—Or Do We?

Companies constantly tell us they have no choice other than to batch. And yes, we agree! We must point out there are times, within our current systems, when batching products or paperwork is more efficient than one-piece flow. Some of you are smiling right now and thinking, "Yes … I knew it!" But ask yourself, "why?" Why do we all have this proclivity to want to batch? We all do it! Why do we all believe it's more efficient? Why is it so difficult to do one-piece flow?

As I stated earlier, we now know the answer to that question … To date, we have discovered eight reasons, or what we consider root causes, as to why people—all of us—have this insatiable appetite to batch* (see Table 6.1).

Batching, in fact, is more efficient than one-piece flow *until* some of the root causes below are addressed. One cannot eliminate the batching until one eliminates the need, or

---

* If you can think of another root cause that can't possibly fit into one of these eight reasons please email me at charlieprotzman@biglean.com.

Table 6.1 The Eight Root Causes of Batching

The Eight Root Causes of Batching with One-Piece Flow Notes
1. Your mind   • Note: We can achieve one-piece flow even with people that don't believe in it, but they have to be forced to do so and will continue to fight you. If they have any opportunity to batch, they will.
2. Setups   • Note: We do not need to eliminate long setup times to achieve one-piece flow. We can do one-piece flow by working around these operations. We normally kanban these parts to the line. However, you cannot reduce the lot size or get to one-piece flow on a piece of equipment until you reduce the setup time.
3. Variation   • Note: We can handle all sorts of variation in one-piece flow implementations. However, the introduction of many new models is a frequent reason shops of all sizes lose one-piece flow.
4. Travel distance   • Note: We must decrease the travel distance or people will batch.
5. Equipment   • Note: We can do one-piece flow by using standard WIP before and after the equipment, i.e., a batch washer or oven.
6. Process   • Note: Here our goal is to use small or smaller batches where it makes sense with a goal of transitioning to continuous flow.
7. Idle time   • Note: We can eliminate the idle time when we implement bumping in a one-piece flow process.
8. Space   • Note: Where there is too much we eliminate it, and where there is too little we add space.

Source: BIG Archives.

the perceived need, for the batching.* They are as follows in prioritized order:

1. Your mind
2. Setups†
3. Variation
4. Travel distance
5. Equipment
6. Process
7. Idle time
8. Space

Let's examine each of these root causes. Please consider that a batching environment can result from one or more of these items.

Your Mind

The single biggest incentive to batch resides in our minds, somewhere very deep in our psyche. Virtually all human beings—no matter what age, no matter how intelligent we are, no matter what environment we are brought up in, or country in which we live—for some reason are "programmed to batch." I honestly believe it is encoded in the fabric of our DNA—it is in our genes, so to speak.

Don't believe me? Have you ever run into people that objected to batching? In our experience, consulting with small firms up to Fortune 100 companies, reviewing hundreds of processes, virtually every single one is designed as a batch

---

* This is similar to what we say about human inspection. You can't get rid of a human inspection step until you eliminate the need for the inspection step i.e., mistake-proofing or 100% automated inspection. Table 6.1 includes notes on where we can do one-piece flow even with the cause forcing the batching.
† Sometimes referred to in other industries as changeovers, turnovers, changing an operating or nurse unit room from one patient to another, taking down and setting up camp, loading and unloading anything from 18-wheelers (trucks) to machines.

process. Between us, the authors have a total of 50 years of hearing objections to implementing one-piece flow. As a result, one can assuredly deduce batching must be an innate quality we all possess, and for some reason, we all seem hardwired to think batching is better. We would argue that if it was not an innate quality, wouldn't all companies just naturally develop one-piece flow systems? After all, one-piece, or continuous, flow is the most efficient way to process almost anything, so why wouldn't we automatically design processes that way?

My claims for this line of thinking are as follows: have you ever had a discussion with someone *not exposed* to one-piece flow (and in many cases it doesn't matter either way) where you did not have to "DEFEND" one-piece flow and work extremely hard to explain why it is better and, in fact, more efficient than batching?

Consider the following analogy. We had a 12-year-old male bichon frise. We only fed him one type of dog food for all those years; except occasionally some white-cake of which he was quite fond of. One day we gave him a big ham bone, which was almost bigger than he was. We had this dog since he was 9 weeks old, and we had never given him a bone. Our dog took this bone and chewed on it for a bit, cleaned off all the meat, and then immediately went down the steps to the backyard and started digging in our garden, where he proceeded to bury the bone, and then came back up the steps. Five minutes later, he went back down the steps to the garden, knew exactly where it was, and dug it up again.

Now, I ask you: why did this dog bury the bone? He had never even seen a bone before, never been trained by his mother to bury a bone, never dug up the dirt in our garden before, and yet he still dug a hole and buried the bone. When he started digging up multiple places to bury it, we finally had to take it away and give him a bath.

So What Is It About, This Batching Thing?

My wife was making maternity clothes for my daughter in law. Her mind kept telling her to batch the patterns. She fought her mind and was then glad she did because she found a mistake in the pattern for the first dress. Otherwise, all the patterns would have been wrong. I believe we are all programmed from birth, just like our dog. None of us were taught to batch, we just come by it naturally. We can't help it. It seems to be an innate human paradigm. This is why one-piece flow is so difficult to sustain, often fails, and why it is so easy to undo after it's been implemented. It is amazing to watch people pilot one-piece flow, finding they even sort of like the new process, but then go right back to batching.

A good friend of mine, Matthias,* who helped us with technical edits to this book, states: "I definitely like this section although I disagree (it is just that I don't believe in hardwired systems). I think it is just a question of mental set-up time. So what we need is a SMED (single minute exchange of dies—or setup reduction) for mental processes to resolve this 'hardwired' stubbornness. People don't like to use their brains if it is not a challenging task/problem we are hardwired. to not lose energy, on not-interesting things, and this ensures our survival. So we try to reduce mental setup times, but, this is a very tentative alternative explanation. Your hardwired argument is just as good. It is just that it reminds me of Chomsky and his whole universal grammar thing, which is hardwired in our brains. After some years, it now turns out that maybe there is no specific hardwired universal grammar."

Authors' Note: *Regardless of what we each individually believe, the authors feel this hypothesis is a good basis for ongoing discussion and future research or thesis in the future.*

---

* Email correspondence with Dr. Matthias Thurer, Jinan University, 12/8/2014.

We like to use another analogy we call *leading the horse to water:*

The horse drinks the water—The horse likes the water but then—The horse refuses to drink the water again.

The batching paradigm is always working against us. It is the silent productivity killer. There are no traditional financial metrics to capture the effects of batching* on productivity. In fact, our financial metrics encourage batching with measures like machine utilization, absorption cost accounting standards, earned hours, etc.

Setups/Changeovers

On my first visit to a new client,[†] the president of the company explained to me their need for an external consultant to help resolve the company's delivery problems. The company had a 65% on-time delivery performance and had 154 late confirmed customer orders. After meeting with the president and several management team members, I left for the day with a number of opinions regarding how to solve the problem. Most of their ideas had to do with adding staffing—ranging from shifts, weekends, people to hours. They all had to do with adding cost, but not evaluating the current system.

The next day I spent several hours on the production floor talking with the operators and first-line supervisors. I noticed one of the products on the "late list" was waiting to be finished, yet, a product that was due several weeks later was first

---

* Traditional accounting techniques were brought to industry by Frederick Taylor in the early 1900s, when he took them from the railroads and adapted them as the basis for the cost accounting principles we have today. Overhead absorption, 100% machine utilization, the concept of earning labor, labor variances, etc. are all enemies to implementing one-piece flow. Traditional accounting systems were designed around batch-based processes to support batching and are still taught in all business schools today! Lean accounting is just starting to make some inroads into companies.

[†] Story furnished by Mike Meyers via personal correspondence dated 1/4/2015.

in line for the same machine. I asked the supervisor, "Why are you doing this?" He told me they had to batch because that was the only way they could keep up. I found that to be an interesting comment when they were 154 jobs behind. I started to investigate why they batched and how we could, if not eliminate the problem, at least minimize it.

It was determined that the reason they batched was because of the 4–6 hours it took to change over the machine. We were very quickly able to video and review the process with their people. We were able to reduce the changeover time by over 50% after the first review. Within 8 weeks we had reduced it to 20 minutes and eliminated all the delinquent orders. Instead of adding staff, we were actually able to produce more parts with fewer personnel.* We reduced our quoted lead times by over 50%, which enabled us to grow the business.

Setups are the second largest driver of batch thinking. There are setups all around us, some of which you may recognize immediately. Setups occur on the racetrack ... pit stops; on major league football fields ... changeover from defense to offense, or to special teams; on baseball fields ... changeover between teams coming up to bat and taking the field; all around our homes and offices we have changeovers ... even as simple a process as loading paper in the copy machine or printer is a setup.

Changeover is defined as the amount of time it takes to set up, or change over, part of a line, an entire line, an area, or a piece of equipment from the last processed piece until the first good piece. The longer the changeover, the more inventories are required to buffer the changeover. Long changeovers usually drive us toward batching larger and larger lot sizes. People will always tell me, "Well, because it takes so long to set it up, it's faster to run all of the same style piece through, before I have to change it back over again." Therefore, the longer the

---

* No one was laid off.

setup or changeover time, the larger the batches of product we must run at one time. The economic order quantity formula was created to calculate the most efficient batch size based on the setup times. With one-piece flow, we no longer have a need for this formula.

Fact: We must reduce setup times before moving to one-piece flow for these areas. Failure to do so will result in missed production targets and has cost people their jobs!

The concept of setup reduction has been around since the early 1900s, but an engineer named Dr. Shigeo Shingo coined the term SMED,* which stands for single minute exchange of dies. Dies are used in manufacturing presses in order to create a pattern or shape of the part being pressed. A simple example of a die in a kitchen would be a cookie cutter shape or changing over a tip on an icing pastry bag. However, it is important to note setup times do not just occur in die changes on presses. A setup can occur simply by unloading and loading parts in a machine during production of a "lot" of parts. Now we introduce the concept of *internal time*. Internal time is the time the machine is down during a setup. This is like the time a racecar is down during a pit stop. This concept extrapolates to any device or machine that is down and waiting for us to unload and load it. *External time* is used to prepare for the pit stop while the car is going around the track, or while the machine is running.

Focus should be on separating internal and external setup times, while converting as much internal time to external setup as possible, then streamlining the setup process as much as or however you can. Setups can always be improved! Small lot production with a goal of one-piece flow requires short setup times allowing us to be more flexible to our customers. Setup time reduction of 50%–90% or more is common in our implementations.

---

* *A Revolution in Manufacturing: The SMED System*, Shigeo Shingo © 1985 Productivity Press.

Let's take the pastry bag example. Imagine you are icing cup cakes and have several colors: blue, red, yellow, black, etc. You need to change over from one color to another. So what will you do? You will use the first color on all the cupcakes and then you have to change over the pastry bag to the next color. How do you do this? You have to take off the tip, squeeze out all the excess into a bowl (in case you need to use it again) or trash can, and then wash it out, and then mix up the new color and put it in the pastry bag. How could you improve the process. One way would be to have 4 different pastry bags; one for each color. I expect some of you do this already. Then you could ice each cupcake one at a time.

Fact: Long setup times drive us to schedule larger and larger batches, driving space required for large amounts of WIP, tying up cash flow, reducing inventory turns, and driving up costs. Batching is the silent productivity killer!

Variation

Variation in processes drives batch production. It is not unusual to hear, "Well, we used to have an assembly line." When asked what happened to it, employees normally say something to the tune of, "the product mix kept growing and they did not know how to handle all the options anymore." There are many process variations that force us to batch: i.e., wherever adjusting is required, trial and error building occurs, we tune or tweak the product, or rework exists. The reason we batch on these occasions is normally because we don't know how to handle it or how to design it in a one-piece flow format.

Fact: Variation was often to blame when one-piece flow assembly lines were abandoned.

Sometimes it is just easier for people to go back to batching. One-piece flow takes work, perseverance, continuous improvement, and following standards in order to sustain it.

Don't discount the hard work required to develop a system designed to continuously improve and raise our standards.

Today's culture is replete with examples of lowering standards: educational testing, veracity of the media, public debate, accountability of government officials, ethics, etc. One's self, one's boss, one's peers, and one's employees are immersed, daily, in a cultural trend designed to continuously lower our standards. It is so much easier to lower our standards than to put forth the work and effort required to raise our standards, whether they be social, academic, government, or industrial. One-piece flow requires adherence to strict standards and then continuous improvement to sustain and fight what we call complacency disease.

Fact: Complacency is like a virus. It starts off slow and continues to grow and multiply. The more successful we become, the easier it is to be more complacent. Renowned British executive Sir John Harvey Jones said, "If you are not progressing, you are regressing."

We have found that many companies are forced to batch due to significant variation in their manufacturing processes. We have even run into cases where the variation was so bad, it was difficult, but not impossible, to set up a one-piece flow line. We have been able to successfully set up and balance lines with high variation using some of the line balancing techniques that we will describe later in the book. We are always working to design out some or all the process variation (i.e., tweaking, tuning, etc.), but sometimes it requires major investments in requalification or testing. Listed below are other types of variation:

1. Variation shows up due to poor engineering practices where the "old craft mentality" surfaces. This mentality is apparent when an operator has to have a certain "feel" based on his/her experience to assemble the part or make the part work. We've all heard these comments before, "Jamie's an artist with that machine," or "Jenny

has that special sense when she just knows the product is ready." This reminds me of the master Scotch taster who knows exactly when the whiskey barrel is ready to tap.

Sometimes this "feel" means hitting it with a hammer, and other times it shows up when the product has to be "shimmed"; this leads, again, to what we call "trial and error" type builds. We see it where engineering has designed in "tweaking" or in-line manual tests. It is especially apparent in very small lot, high mix product lines. The variation also occurs in high-technology manufacturing with large amounts of touch labor.

2. We also see variation with constant part shortages caused by class B and below manufacturing resource planning systems, or where vendor deliveries, or parts, are lost in the stockroom. Sometimes inadequate vendor part packaging, container sizes, or even minimum lot requirements can cause batching and overproduction.

3. Variation occurs, when operators are responsible for obtaining their own materials, as the operators often need to search for parts prior to starting a work order. We find that sometimes people even steal parts from other lines.

4. Another example is when operators are forced to perform material handling activities, such as removing bearings from small plastic bags and unwrapping parts placed in boxes full of peanuts, to have parts for use on the line.

Fact: In most cases, one can implement one-piece flow, regardless of the variation in the line. We have yet to find a line or transactional process where we could not apply one-piece flow once the reasons for batching were eliminated and in some cases where they had not been eliminated, i.e., high-mix with extremely low-volume lines. It helps to overcome these barriers to enable the conversion to one-piece flow, which is the more efficient process with long-term sustainability.

Travel Distance

Whenever you introduce travel distance into an operation, no matter how small, whether it is for the product or operator, you drive batching.

Why do we only go to the supermarket about once a week or maybe less? Most of us are going to purchase all the food items we think we will need for the next week. In fact, if you go to Sam's Club, BJ's, or Costco, you are purchasing more than a week's worth at a time, sometimes several months.

Let me ask you … how often would you go to the store and purchase only one day's worth of groceries? That would be crazy, wouldn't it? Yet, what happens when we buy more than we need? Over time it expires, gets freezer burn, and goes bad. Next, we find we have to buy another freezer and/ or refrigerator to store all the extra groceries. How many of you have not seen the bottom of your freezer for some time where all that food is hidden by other food that we got such a good deal on?

"So what?" you say. Well, if we overbought or even went to a restaurant a couple of times that week, we may find we have to scrap half the groceries. But at least we don't have to make that trip back to the store for a while, right? Come to think of it, how long does fresh produce or deli meats last? Do you ever find your deli meats have spoiled? Nothing like having to smell the bag each time before you eat it, huh? How long does milk last … about a week or so, right? So, now that I think about it, I guess I have to go to the store about once a week anyway. Now I'm starting to wish I hadn't bought the 100-pack of toilet paper at Sam's Club and then, after filling every bathroom to the brim, search for space to store the rest of it.

To apply this concept to the simple replenishment of materials: the longer the travel distance, the more it drives us to fill the parts bins to the rim. Sometimes we will fill them even over the designated "water level" to avoid refilling them so often. Similarly, in the office, people will stash loads of office supplies at their desks so they don't have to get up to keep visiting the supply cabinet, which then triggers purchasing to waste money buying more supplies, thinking they have been depleted.

I love nurses, but even they will tell you, they are the most serious offenders of stashing the "things they really need" in their pockets, at the desk, and all over the hospital floor, so the item is convenient to them for when they need it. When we do 5S (workplace organization—Sort, Store, Shine, Standardize, and Sustain) at hospitals, we typically need to lift the jaws of the purchasing and accounting folks off the ground, as they stare in awe at the amount of supplies that were hidden from them.

Fact: The more risk (i.e., variation) perceived as inherent in the system, the larger the batches of inventory we will want to buffer and have at our fingertips. We call this "Just in Case!" inventory.

The longer the distance, the more pieces we want to carry between places, i.e., in parallel, and this makes perfect sense. For example, we may carry multiple parts from one work center or stockroom to another on a cart vs. carrying them one at a time.

Another example closer to home is a firewood delivery. The firewood is often dumped on the driveway, and the homeowner uses a wheelbarrow to move the firewood to the backyard. The homeowner would never carry the firewood, one log at a time, unless there was no access to a wheelbarrow or the pile was very small, in which case he or she would carry as much as they could fit or hold in their arms.

Timeout 4

Take four pens or pencils and place them at the end of a 4×6 table. Then ask for a volunteer to move the items to the other side of the table. You will find they will grab all four and move them as a batch. Ask them why they did not move them one at a time. They will look at you like you are crazy and then answer,

Timeout Exercise #4

- Take four pens or pencils and place them at the end of a 4 x 6 table. Then ask for a volunteer to move the items to the other side of the table.

- Ask them why they did not move them one at a time. *Think if you've heard yourself use this excuse before?*

_____
_____
_____
_____
_____
_____
_____
_____
_____
_____
_____
_____
_____
_____
_____
_____
_____
_____
_____
_____
_____
_____
_____

"Because I had to walk all the way to the other side. Why in the world would I take one at a time?" Indeed! (see Timeout 4).

In a hospital emergency department (ED) process we reduced the wait time to see the provider (doctor or physician assistant) by 80%, by cutting down travel distance and giving the provider two or three designated rooms in which to work. This reduced the waiting time to see an ED doctor from typically 2–10 hours to less than 20 minutes. In the winter at one particular hospital in Florida, 18% of people used to leave before they were able to see the doctor because the wait was so long; now it is less than 1%.*

In factories, the further away the next process or machine is, the more we will want to batch prior to moving to the next operation or step in the process. When we batch like this in one place, it means we normally need to sit, which discourages one-piece flow even more. This is because one-piece flow requires standing and walking operations which, believe it or not, are better for all of us, both ergonomically and from a fitness perspective.

Wow, You're Right

Here's an example that should get every person to stop and go, "wow, you're right." At least that is my hope because then maybe one at a time we can start to change this batching behavior, because I am tired of waiting in line.

When at a wedding, waiting in line at the bar, do you find you ever double up on your order so you don't have to wait in that long line again (see Figure 6.1)? Yet, when you stop to really think about it ... this is one of the main causes the line is so long. What is ironic is that this tendency to double up on our orders at the bar actually makes the rest of those waiting

---

* For more information read *Leveraging Lean in Healthcare*, Protzman, Mayzell, Kerpchar © 2011 CRC Press.

Figure 6.1 Waiting in bar line at a wedding. Because they only had one bar set up, the line was so long everyone kept ordering at least double what they needed so it kept getting longer! (Source: BIG Archives.)

in line behind us wait even longer, driving *them* to double order and thus continually slowing down the line even more with each drink order. I have seen some people order three drinks at a time. Of course, they try to disguise it as a drink for someone else, which, of course, that person turns out not to like. It also causes our drinks to become diluted, therefore adversely changing the product.

As my first whiskey and ginger ale is sitting there melting the ice, the other two I ordered are being poured. I better keep track of the first one poured; if I don't, the last drink I have may be completely watered down by the time I get to it. This causes, and we've all heard it, people to say, "Yeah, they're not pouring drinks as strong as the beginning of the night." Now you can point and say, "No, you batchard, if you had ordered one drink at a time, they would all taste the same!"

Fact: The longer the travel distance the more we will want to stay where we are and continue to batch, prior to traveling to the next step. Batching is the silent productivity killer!

Chapter 7

The Eight Root Causes of Batching Continued ...

Starting off the next half of the Eight Root Causes, understand that one-piece flow examples **do** exist within our everyday world. Think of some chain pizza restaurants; remember the ovens with the large door and giant handle. Remember the long paddle the chefs would use to scoop the pizza out from the back of the oven. What do most of the chain restaurants use now? Next time you're picking up your pizza at Pizza Hut restaurant, take notice of the "flow ovens" in use. Now, think about some of your own processes. Are you using a "one-piece flow conveyor oven," or the "batch oven?" This brings us to our next root cause.

Equipment

Some equipment is designed to operate batch. This means you have to wait until all operations are done on all the parts before you see the first piece.

We worked on one process, which had a machine designed to work on 29 parts at a time. We couldn't figure out why they picked 29? The machine was capable of working on one, or any number, at a time. Meanwhile, as each part is being worked on individually, the rest of the parts sit in a lot delay status until all 29 parts are completed on the machine. Many times this batching is driven by an actual, or perceived, lengthy run-time for the machine. But in actuality, if the fixtures were designed for one-piece flow, the machine time is more than adequate (fast enough) to support one-piece flow. Once the machine run is complete, we have to manage 58 parts all at once (the 29 coming off and going on), not to mention we need the space to accommodate the material handling associated with all of these parts.

At hospitals, labs have to centrifuge patients' blood tubes. Some centrifuges hold up to a hundred or more tubes. So now we're waiting until we fill the centrifuge completely in order to run it. When you expand the impact of the batching throughout the entire lab, think about the potential devastating consequences. In some cases, minutes can mean the difference between life and death.

Because of this, most hospital labs have what is called a "stat" process in order to get the highest priority tubes completed/resulted first. The stat process is handled in smaller lots, with less handoffs, but is traditionally still batched. If our turnaround times on stat tubes or in some cases even non-stat tubes are too long, it can have a significantly negative impact on the patient. When we implement flow processes in laboratories or pharmacies, we eliminate the need to process stat tubes separately. Every patient's blood tubes are processed as stat tubes because there is no longer a need to separate the two flows.*

One company, prior to us working with them, had spent extra money to convert their test equipment from being

---

* *Leveraging Lean in Health Care*, Protzman, Mayzell, Kerpchar © 2011 CRC Press; *Leveraging Lean in Medical Laboratories*, Protzman, Kerpchar, Mayzell © 2015 CRC Press.

able to test one piece at a time to 20 parts at a time. Even though the test time was the same for each piece, it was perceived as a bottleneck because the inventory piled up there. The prevailing thinking at the time was that testing 20 pieces would be faster and more efficient than testing one piece at a time. Converting the machine was very expensive, took up a lot more space, and resulted in even more batching. The machine also broke down all the time and had parts waiting to be tested both inside and outside it, and the operator had to stand at the machine all day while it tested the parts. They had all this space tied up, which they called a "parts hotel."

Once the analysis was done, we verified they only needed one part testing at a time in order to meet the cycle time of the line. It was not a bottleneck after all. We then trained them in one-piece flow, and we created standard work in process (WIP) in front of and after the test set. After a year or so, they spent thousands of dollars to design and convert the machine back to single-piece flow. Now the standard WIP is gone.

It is not uncommon for a person to think bigger is better, and more is more, and processing more parts in equipment at the same time means saving money. People refer to this thinking as the benefits that come with "economies of scale." Contrary to popular belief, more often than not, running things one at a time will be your most cost-efficient way to go.

We have seen many batch types of computer numerical control (CNC) machine shop equipment (see Figure 7.1). At one plant, they have a milling machine that batches eight parts at a time. After the operator loads the parts, the machine selects a tool from the carousel and performs an operation using a tombstone* on up to eight pieces at a time. The machine then selects the next tool, and performs the next operation on all

---

* A tombstone is a loading fixture for a milling CNC machine.

Figure 7.1 Batching equipment CNC fixture. Uses one tool on each part then switches to the next tool for each part. (From BIG Archives.)

the pieces, etc. Extra inspection occurs before and after the machining operation because the operators don't trust the machine. The end result is you don't get the first piece until the entire batch is completed, and if one piece is defective they all will most likely be defective, just like our "cookie example." The problem is that this is the way the manufacturer designed the equipment. If it had been one-piece flow we would not have needed extra WIP in place to buffer the machine. In addition, when the machine broke a tool, all the pieces were bad or had to be reworked.

The food service industry utilizes many batch pieces of food service equipment, such as ovens and mixers. It may also employ a process known as the cook-chill process. Cook-chill heats the food to high temperatures, quickly chills it, bags and seals it, so it can then be stored in a refrigerator for up to 28 days. The online definition of this process states, "The cook-chill process lends itself to batch cooking in large quantities of product for storage and future use or for distribution to multiple food service outlets. The equipment necessary for this process includes cook tanks, a pump and fill station and chilling equipment,"* in addition to the probable need for more walk-in refrigerator space. The result was embodied in what one might not necessarily consider "fresh" and "appetizing," as more often than not, the hospital overcooked the food, or it came out very, very watery.

Looking back to the office environment, if you folks think you're immune to this type of batching; a lot of office equipment used to be batched. Remember the copier machines with sorters on the side? In the early copiers you had to run each page of the set separately, for instance 100 pages of each one, then put them in stacks, collate them, and then finally staple them. The next innovation added a sheet feeder, which would take each page, create 10 copies, one for each sorter, and then take the next page, etc., until you had 10 complete sets. After that, you would have to remove each stack, and then staple it, and then wait for the next run. The next innovation added the stapling, although it never seemed to staple in the right place.

However, many times the copiers would get stuck or break down in the middle of the run. This forced the user to remove all the stacks and then try to figure out where to start the copier again or just trash them all and start over. Today's copiers scan in the paperwork and then make complete or collated sets with a stapling option.

A simple everyday example is an elevator vs. an escalator. When you think about it, the elevator is batch vs. the escalator, which is continuous flow. I know which one I'd rather be stuck on if there were a power failure.

Fact: Batching type equipment forces you to wait until the batch is complete, creating more inventories in the system. They force us to stack up material before and after the batch type equipment. If one part is defective then all are defective. Batching is the silent productivity killer!

---

* http://www.designprocessinc.com/cook_chill.html. Authors' note: there are some applications where this process may be beneficial, i.e., for soups and packaging for sale in stores, etc.

Processes

Some processes are naturally batch type processes, like foundries, which make iron, steel, or aluminum. These processes are not unlike those you can observe in home cooking and restaurants. We find similar processes in powered plastics, metal manufacturing, and Food and Drug Administration (FDA) or biotechnology processes (see Figure 7.2). Many biotechnology companies have "kitchens," where they will produce buffer solutions to save time in mixing final solutions. We end up eliminating this buffer stock and make the recipes from scratch. Some work processes are batch, such as central receiving areas, or where there may be a need to do "offline operations."

Drug companies are now finding the advantages of moving to smaller batch sizes via continuous manufacturing. Less space, smaller equipment, less WIP, less waste, and the ability to service smaller, more specialized areas with lower volume requirements are all benefits of moving to smaller lots. Equipment is cheaper and more portable and/or flexible and once the layout/footprint is established can be more easily and more economically transplanted to other, normally smaller, facilities in other countries. The advent of analytical

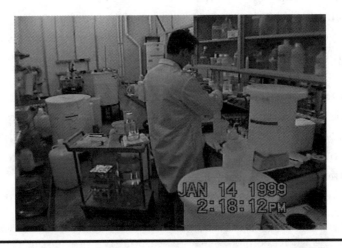

Figure 7.2 Batch process. Biotech industry. (From BIG Archives.)

technology designed to measure drug properties is continually enabling the transition to smaller and smaller lots for drug companies.*

I had a client[†] that was struggling with the "uptime" in their pouring process; the uptime in this casting process was 60%. As we studied the problem, the team suggested many solutions ranging from adding equipment to adding a transfer operator to developing a heated transfer system. After much analysis, we finally ended up reducing the batch size of iron transferring to the pouring stations. By reducing the batch size, we were able to reduce wasted iron by 30% and improve uptime to 90% with no capital or staffing increases.

Fact: Converting to one-piece flow is not always possible with the technology that exists today, which is why sometimes we have to default to small lot vs. one-piece flow. Batch processing would still fall into the small lot category. All the risks associated with batching are engrained in natural batch type processes. We need to keep working on technology, which reduces the need for these batch type processes. It should be noted that all high-volume food processes are one-piece flow.

Batching is the silent productivity killer!

Idle Time

Okay, this one is crucial to your understanding—idle time drives batching. That's right: people who are idle will find ways to batch. If you don't believe me, stand and observe someone who is idle. Almost no one likes to be idle, especially if his or her boss is watching. If someone is idle on their

---

* Based on a conversation with Dr. Steve Klohr. Also see article "Real Time Monitoring," cen.acs.org, 11/24/ 2014.
† Story furnished by Mike Meyers via personal correspondence 1/4/2015.

job they may find tasks to do that typically reinforce batch practices and will potentially do unnecessary work, or work before it is needed, which is considered overproduction; the most common of the eight wastes.*

Fact: Excess inventory and idle time are always signs of problems.

Humans generally like to keep busy. Most employees, if left alone, will continue working, and if it's possible to make something at their station, they will continue to build. If you're a manager and reading this book, you're telling yourself now to put this book down: "how can the authors tell me they don't want my idle workers to remain busy?" In fact, that's not what we are saying at all. If an office or shop floor worker/operator is running at a faster cycle time than the person they are feeding, then they will continue to make parts and "bury" the person in WIP, rather than sit idle.

This is where the concept of the "in-line process kanban" or "WIP caps" was developed (see Figure 7.3). In order to "not bury" the person we are feeding, the operators were told to only build until the kanban square was full, whether it is one-piece or up to the calculated WIP cap quantity. Generally, most operators ignore the WIP cap quantity and continue to build until there is no more room for any parts in the space available.

This behavior is especially apparent in "sit-down–station-balanced" lines; thus, "sit-down" lines embrace and help drive batching behaviors. When employees sit, they don't "flex" and help out other operators. This phenomenon where some workers are idle and then bury each other with WIP is especially prevalent in these types of lines.

Batching is the silent productivity killer!

* Based on the seven wastes from the Toyota Production System normally credited to Ohno Taiichi.

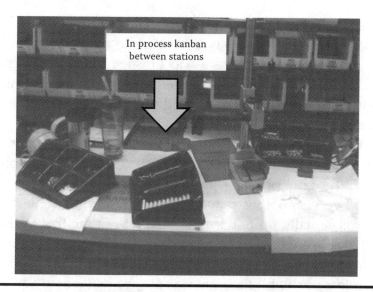

Figure 7.3 In-process kanban between stations. When this company converted from batch to flow by eliminating the "station balanced" sit-down positions, and in-process kanbans between each station, and implemented baton zone line balancing, they realized a 63% improvement in productivity on this line alone! This company had been doing Lean for 15 years with a certified Lean Master, followed all the company Lean teachings and practices, and thought they had reached their limit on improvement. Over 16 weeks of this new Lean thinking across 14 lines, they freed up 14 people—all temps—who they let go. (From BIG Archives.)

Freddie's Story

At company X, there were two operators we filmed doing the same job. Our goal was to put together standard work for the job. The product runs down an assembly line, and the operators are supposed to work between the first two stations. There were, however, up to five stations they could access. The first task was to place a gasket on top of the product at the first station. The second task was to move to the second station (while the machine was filling the first product at the first station) and pick up a piece of chalk and write the next sequential number on the product and then put the chalk down. The next task was to pick up a rod and check a pipe in the product at the second station to make sure it was filled properly. The final task was to go back to the first product station and, immediately as it was finished filling, to cover the holes in the product. Covering the holes was a critical task and if not done immediately could result in defects to the product.

A different person, of course, trained each operator, and the supervisor stood by watching each operator do the job differently; more on this later. The first shift operator, Tank, worked very smoothly, repeating each step in the same order, and was actually waiting for the final task at the first station each cycle as necessary in his walk pattern. The fill time for the products varied, and some filled faster than others. Regardless of the fill time, he was always ready and waiting to cover the holes as required. His wait time ranged from 4 seconds to 11 seconds but this was ok and to be built into the standard work.

The second operator, Freddie, did his walk pattern differently. We watched as Freddie's first step was to pick up five gaskets and then proceed to set the first gasket on the first product at station one. So far so good. Then he went to station two and did his pipe check, picked up the chalk, and wrote down the number. Note, this was a different order of sequence than the first operator. Then, Freddie picked up the other four gaskets and proceeded to walk down the line and place them on the products from station two to four. However, even though he rushed back to the first station, he didn't make it back in time to cover the holes as required. We watched the video as the supervisor just stood there and shook his head in disgust but never said anything to Freddie. Freddie, then, continued this behavior and was always rushed, very busy, and tired at the end of the day.

After watching the video with Freddie and the supervisor we asked Freddie why he would grab multiple gaskets and batch them. He looked at us quizzically. He said that he thought it was more efficient and that otherwise he would be idle waiting at station one. This way he was always busy, and if there were ever a problem, he would have some extra time to fix it. No one ever explained to him the reason why it was critical to cover the holes immediately at station one. It was interesting to note that even though the supervisor was watching and was disgusted every time Freddie was late getting back to station one, he didn't realize what Freddie was doing wrong because there was no standard work in place. He would just get disgusted and shake his head all the time.

So, we started explaining what batching was and then asked Freddie—if he had 30 sandwiches to make, how would he make them? He looked at us funnily and said, "Well I would lay out 30 pieces of bread, and then put on the lettuce on each one, and then tomato on each one etc." We asked him if he believed one-piece flow would be faster and he said "no way man!" Expecting this answer, we said, "Freddie, imagine if you had not eaten in three days ... I am now going to make you a sandwich, and you have to watch me. The first thing I do is lay out 30 pieces of bread on the counter. What are you going to say to me?" Freddie said; "You better hurry up with those sandwiches." We all laughed. I said, "Now you have to wait until the last one is done until you are going to get yours."

We asked Freddie, "What would be a better way to do it?" He said, "Make them one at a time and then I will get mine right away." I couldn't control myself: "Exactly! Can you think of anywhere they make sandwiches one at a time?" Freddie said, "Subway, Quiznos, Which-Which? all make their sandwiches one-piece flow." We discussed the advantages of one-piece flow using the examples *he provided us*. We showed Freddie Tank's video and how Tank was working one-piece flow, was never rushed, and was always ready in time to cover the holes; in fact, he had idle time. Now that he provided input, understood the concept, and felt included, Freddie said, "I get it, and I will start doing it this way." We thanked Freddie for his time and for his ideas, and he went back to work.

The next day Freddie came in to us after his shift and said, "I tried not batching yesterday, and it worked out pretty well. For the first time in a long time, I was not tired at the end of the day. I was always on time to cover the holes, and I even got a little rest between cycles. This one-piece flow stuff really works!"

When we come across scenarios where employees are idle in companies, we hunt for the "why." We know that it's next to impossible to have zero idle time on a shift, whether it's due to equipment down, or a holdup somewhere in the line … as the saying goes, *downtime happens.* The key point here is finding out if the downtime is a "special cause"* incident or whether it is "common cause." If it is in fact due to special cause, we teach the employees to use idle time valuably. Rather than trying to "get ahead" of the next step in the process, we need to look for what can be improved in your station or work area. Idle time can also be used for cross training. More times than not, what was thought of as "special cause," happens three times a shift, every shift, every day, and now we realize these special causes are really common causes that must be addressed. At many companies we recommend supervisors develop a list of what workers can do if they are idle for 1 minute, 5 minutes, 10 minutes, 1 hour, etc. This way, if the line experiences idle time, the workers have a plan of action instead of sitting there idle waiting for someone to tell them what to do next.

Fact: Because of our innate tendencies to want to keep busy, especially if our supervisor is watching, we will find ways to do it (batch).

---

* "A fault in the interpretation of observations, seen everywhere, is to suppose that every event (defect, mistake, accident) is attributable to someone (usually the nearest at hand), or is related to some special event, i.e., special cause variation. The fact is that most troubles with service and production lie in the system, i.e., common cause variation. Sometimes the fault is indeed local, attributable to someone on the job or not on the job when he should be. We speak of *faults of the system as common causes* of trouble, and *faults from fleeting events as special causes.*" W. Edwards Deming.

Space

Space in the work environment is extremely important to manage, as too little or too much can lead to batching. Let's examine when we have too much space first (see Figure 7.4). In this case, we tend to batch because we have surplus table or floor space to store the extra inventory. We have found that providing more space than required encourages batching and, at a minimum, embraces the accumulation of items not needed, i.e., junk/clutter.

At one company, operators complained incessantly, for over a week, that we did not provide enough space in the layout. When we pointed out, time and time again, that they didn't need any more space to get the job done at their workstations, the employees complained to the Human Resources (HR) department. HR (who did not understand one-piece flow at the time) met with us and *ordered* us to provide additional tables in order to keep the workers happy. We met with the line employees to advise them of this and they were thrilled they had "won" the battle and gotten their extra table back. We put the table back in the work area that night.

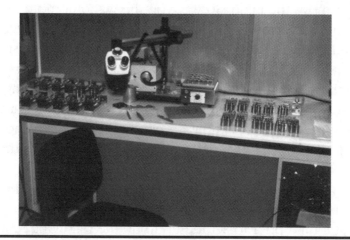

Figure 7.4 Batching. Too much space. How much space does the operator really need? (From BIG Archives.)

Figure 7.5 Batch workstation. Gave the operator more space and then just filled it up with more WIP! (BIG Archives.)

The following morning there was so much "junk" on the table, in terms of tools and extra parts, that the line was completely out of balance, and the operators were complaining they had "less" room to work and demanded yet another table (see Figure 7.5). HR representatives visited the line and, observing the new table fraught with "junk," they now understood our perspective and agreed with us. They told us we could remove the table. So we won the war, but more importantly, after explaining the situation further, the employees realized the fault in their reasoning and welcomed the smaller table space.

By the same token, *too little* space can create batching as well. When we don't have enough space, we tend to batch in the space we have, simply because we don't have enough room to lay out the materials, tools, and equipment in the proper order necessary to flow the process. If there is no space, you have to batch, as you restrict the access to the parts. This forces the operators to batch one or two operations at a time prior to setting up to do the following required operations. Converting to one-piece flow will free up space (see Figure 7.6).

Figure 7.6   Room for growth. Space freed up in a factory after implementing one-piece flow on just two lines. (From BIG Archives.)

Fact: Did you know that space in layouts is one of the single biggest causes of waste in our companies, whether manufacturing, health care or office based (see Figure 7.7). However, batching is still the root cause of the poor layout and need for excess space. Whenever you create a batch-based layout, you have to leave room for all the WIP. This then creates travel distance and piles of inventory. Whenever you leave space for inventory you can be sure people will fill it up. It is amazing to see how fast empty space gets filled up with excess WIP, proving, yet again, that batching is the silent productivity killer!

Figure 7.7   Batch layout. Electronics factory. (From BIG Archives.)

Timeout 5

Go back through all eight reasons batching occurs and make a list of times where you or your company have batched, even if you want to look at your personal day-to-day activities. Save this list for a later exercise (see Timeout 5).

Why We Batch and Why It Hurts Our Company

The concept of batching initially seems logical and sensible until one is taught and truly understands the one-piece flow paradigm. Operating a line using a batch process takes up significant amounts of valuable resources, time, space, and inventory (cash). Batching can lead to a lack of overall process controls, lack of standardization, and poor quality (95%–99% good parts). If a defect occurs, it is not discovered until the end of the process, where the entire batch ends up defective (see Figure 7.8).

With one-piece flow, we can discover the defect immediately after the first piece is completed, and, in a truly one-piece flow system, we never hand off a bad part to the

Figure 7.8   Defective batch. MRB stands for material review board. (From BIG Archives.)

Timeout Exercise #5

- Go back through our eight reasons batching occurs and make a list of ten times where you or your company have batched, even in your day-to-day activities.

I. _____

II. _____

III. _____

IV. _____

V. _____

VI. _____

VII. _____

VIII. _____

IX. _____

X. _____

- *Save this list for a later exercise*

next station. One significant benefit of one-piece flow is the applicability to implement inspection at the source with successive checks and the use of creative mistake-proofing devices.

Bulk Discounts

When we purchase a product in a large quantity, we expect a discount. We like to call it "buying in bulk," but really, it's batching and hoarding. This concept has spilled over into the manufacturing process and further gives credit to those embracing batch.

They rationalize; it must be more efficient to produce in batch, because otherwise the firm would not offer quantity discounts. So we all are programmed to order or buy more than we need, and before we need it, in order to save costs. I now pose the question; do these "bulk/batch" discounts really save our companies or us money in the long run? Ironically, GAAP, or generally accepted accounting principles, support batching ... after all, isn't inventory considered an "asset" on the balance sheet? In reality, in the one-piece flow world, we look at any excess inventory as a liability.

Okay, let's get to some reader involvement: raise your hand if you shop at a Costco, Sam's Club, or similar type store as discussed earlier. Now that your hand is raised, ask yourself this next set of financial questions:

- How many of you had to purchase an extra refrigerator or freezer and find a larger pantry to store the 3 months' worth of groceries and sundries you are purchasing?
- How many of you have food in your cupboards, fridge, or at the bottom of your freezer 6 months to a year old?
- How often have you purchased something at the local store that you had already purchased at the big-box store but didn't have time to check or forgot you already had it?

- How much money do you have tied up in inventory? If you bought it on a credit card you may be paying interest on it as well.

Timeout 6

Many of us shop at big-box stores like Costco or Sam's Club. List any times that you have "bought in bulk" in business, only to find out that this caused a need for more inventory, caused you to purchase more than needed, or you later found parts that you had bought long ago that had now expired or were obsolete (see Timeout 6).

This principle applies to businesses as well. From the supply chain point of view, discounts create artificial demand that defeats our ability to level-load the factory schedule. There is a cost to purchasing quantity before you need it. In the factory, when the Marketing/Sales department offers a discount or promotion, the factory employees must work around the clock and receive overtime to get the product out. Then, when the sale is over, the factory has to cut back hours or even lay off some employees. This "artificial demand" is a byproduct of batching. This has the effect of squeezing gross margins in a vise between the top sales line with the discount and the increasing cost of the goods sold line due to overtime, which impacts our overall bottom line.

We have seen companies with stockrooms or shelves full of finished goods that were the result of large quantity runs (batching). The theory was that as long as the machine is set up then all these extra pieces are considered "free." We just have to store them until someone calls us, or maybe we can rework them and deliver them quicker than starting from scratch. However, most of the time the calls never come! And no one checks to see if any can be reworked, because it takes too much time. We must either allocate or create space, like building mezzanines (see Figure 7.9), for all this inventory,

Timeout Exercise #6

- Many of us shop at big-box stores like Costco or Sam's Club. List any times that you have "bought in bulk" in business, only to find that in doing so you caused a need for more inventory, purchased more than needed, or found parts you bought long ago that are now expired or obsolete.

I. _____

II. _____

III. _____

IV. _____

V. _____

VI. _____

VII. _____

VIII. _____

IX. _____

X. _____

Figure 7.9 This company had so much extra inventory they stored it in 19 mezzanines all across the factory. Some even had smiley faces on them. The accountants shut the factory down and counted these parts every 3 months. Most of these parts had "birthdays" because no one ever wanted to climb up and get them. So they all became excess and obsolete. But the thinking at the time was they were "free," because they were already set up to run the parts! (From BIG Archives.)

that was built way before we needed it, and may not have even had orders for it. Sometimes we build inventory just to keep people busy. The parts sit, collecting dust, and quickly become "excess and obsolete." Whenever we make more than we need we often have to sell it at a discounted price, which is another hidden cost.

The exceptions to this rule are stores similar to Wal-Mart that offer discounts every day, or like Joseph A. Banks, which has sales all the time, which in essence "level-loads" their demand.

Batchards?

We have affectionately coined the politically incorrect term "batchards" to describe people displaying this batching behavior or mindset. We define batchards as those who have been introduced to one-piece flow principles but refuse to follow them, even in situations where it has been proven to be the best method. These are the "stuck in the mud types" that won't give up batching, no matter what. They will batch in defiance of any authority and smile at you while they are doing it. You can hear them thinking, "You want me to stop? Come and make me!" These people aren't bad, but their batching behavior is!

Parent-Teacher Association (PTA) volunteers at an elementary school published the school's newsletters. They copied, collated, and distributed it to the children. The volunteers always batched this process. First they made 300 copies of each of the five or six pages. They put each page of the newsletter in a separate stack on the conference room table. Each volunteer would go around the table and collate one set of the five or six pages, which has now become one newsletter, and place them in a stack. Then they would all pick up newsletters, again from several stacks, and staple and fold them together, and then place them in yet another stack.

You can begin to imagine how much room these stacks took up and why the PTA needed to book the entire conference room. Then they stuffed the newsletters in envelopes and placed them in yet another stack. However, they never stayed in neat stacks, especially once they were folded. The stacks tended to lean and sometimes would even fall off the table. Lastly, the volunteers would take the envelopes to the classrooms before dismissal time and hand them to the teachers, who would distribute them to the children.

One day the volunteers arrived late, and one of them, my wife, suggested they do one-piece flow. She had suggested this several times before to no avail. Each time they refused, because they said it would not be as efficient. However, in this emergency case and after much discussion, which made their available time even shorter, they decided to try one-piece flow.

While they still made the stacks of each page, they now set up an assembly line where one person would grab one from each stack, someone else would staple and fold, and someone else would stuff the envelopes.

Sometimes they would have each person do their own from start to finish. We call this the rabbit chase method. Surprisingly, even to the most skeptical volunteer, they got them done so much faster that all of the children received their newsletters from the moms in the hallway just as they were leaving.

Afterwards, all the volunteers begrudgingly agreed this would have been impossible if they had done it the old (batch) way, but some actually liked the new way because it took up less space, it eliminated all those extra stacks, and nothing fell off the table. Interestingly enough, in the future, they reverted to doing it the batch way when my wife was not there. When my wife was there and insisted on one-piece flow, they (the batchards) proudly exclaimed, "We didn't do it this way the last time when you weren't here."

Why do we do this? This is an example of our "leading the horse to water" analogy in Chapter 6.

When Do We Batch?

If we have not been introduced to one-piece flow the answer is, generally, we batch whenever humanly possible. Let me explain to you how I know this.

We have found during initial one-piece flow assessments that many companies think their product lines are one-piece flow; yet, as we stated earlier, we constantly see batching within and throughout the lines. In some cases they would tell you they have been doing one-piece flow for years or even decades; but they still do not realize they are batching within their lines or offices. They honestly think their lines are one-piece flow and are proud to show them off to customers.

It is not unusual to see batching at companies touted as "world-class" as part of tours given by various trade organizations. They think their lines are "flowing," when in reality, they are nowhere close to the level of flow possible. Some companies have even told us, "We have improved enough," or they have already finished implementing their one-piece flow initiative and, "You can't possibly think there is anything you can help us with!"

The Batching Paradigm Impact

Batch environments create the perception that more space and more people are needed. The reason we need extra space is for all that inventory (WIP), and when companies batch, typically each person is working separately on one machine. If you watch them you find most of their time is idle and spent watching the machine. This is flawed thinking and clearly not efficient, and this is not thinking one-piece flow.

In a batch environment, if people have a choice they will always take the easiest thing to work on first. In some cases we have seen customer orders postponed, and in extreme cases pushed out longer than a year, because their orders were "harder" or more complex to produce than the other orders in the backlog.

It is kind of like an emergency room triage process, but in reverse. The harder orders (patients) wait, while the easiest and least risky orders (patients) get done first. Normally, this is because companies need the cash flow, or they have to make the numbers for the end of the month. I'm sure you've never been in a scenario where a manager wanted a "number" met no matter what the cost. How will you handle this differently in the future?

We also batch when we "don't have a choice," and batching is mandated by our policies and procedures. Many times batching gets written into ISO9000 procedures, and then ISO procedures are used as an excuse not to do one-piece flow. In reality, all we have to do is change our procedures to reflect our new one-piece flow process. We have even had military agencies remove lot-testing restrictions once they saw we had our processes under control with one-piece flow.

One company had a president who absolutely refused to believe in one-piece flow. When he bought out another company, which had been working on one-piece flow for several years, he forced them to return to building in 10-piece lots (batches), whether they needed them or not. He didn't care about inventory turns and had several buildings where he stored the "just in case" raw material and WIP inventory. He knew it cost more but didn't care, because he had a huge markup on his product. He was actually proud to show off all his buildings full of inventory, just in case it was needed.

Delivery and performance scores dropped while inventory turns increased after he took over the company. More space was required, and the workforce morale plummeted. Their former competitors "batched" worse than they did, and as a result they either bought their competitors or agreed to produce this product for their competitors. This was the only reason they survived. They did have an excellent product for which they are now the only source and can charge a premium for the product.

Just imagine if a company in this same position had continued with one-piece flow and continued to improve, instead of falling back on batching habits. How much money could they have made (and then shared with their employees!)?

We see this scenario over and over again, where it is so easy to lose one-piece flow when a company is bought out or a new leader emerges without a background in one-piece flow. More times than not, they refuse to change. Even when pointing out the advantages to one-piece flow, this company president was too firmly entrenched in his batch production mentality to change.

Fact: Often we have to make the difficult argument, "We know you are making money now; but just think of how much money you could be making." Successful companies are the most vulnerable to complacency but don't normally discover it until it is too late.

Chapter 8

What Problems Come with the Batching Paradox?

The One-Piece Flow Paradox

One-piece flow is initially totally counterintuitive for just about all of us, which leads us to somewhat of a paradox. Once you "get" the one-piece flow paradigm, everything necessary to support and sustain one-piece flow makes perfect sense. In fact (and it is so odd to experience this over and over again), once people "get it," they ironically are unable to comprehend why no one else seems to "get it," because now, to them, it seems like common sense.*

It takes an awakening or epiphany, some event or situation, to trigger each of us to "get it."† Most of us who have "gotten it," can remember back to the trigger; video, book,

---

* In the consulting trade, this is where we say if you can convert a concrete (batch) head into the one-piece flow mindset, they tend to become zealots. Kind of like someone who just quits smoking.

† "Getting it" refers to someone finally realizing and seeing how one-piece flow is truly better than batching and finally converting their thinking as well as actions to the new one-piece flow paradigm.

Figure 8.1 Batching Super Hero: Lean Man with his ever-running video camera. (Source: BIG Archives. Designed and used with permission. Joe and Ed Markiewiez, Ancon Gear. First published in the *Lean Practitioner's Field Book*, © 2015 CRC Press.)

benchmarking another company, training session, etc. Sometimes, maybe it took all of these to eventually help us see the light. If you are like me, you know that once we "got it," "it" was so clear and bright.

Sadly, some of us will never "get it." Not everyone can let go of the batching paradigm. For some it is so engrained and so comfortable to do things the way they have always done it before. Interestingly enough, if you can convert a batchard* you will find, once they "get it," they become one-piece flow Super Heroes. It's as if Clark Kent shed the suit and tie and brandished a "one-piece flow" or an "L" on his chest, ready to leap long assembly lines or across office desks in a single bound (see Figure 8.1).

---

* Batchard is the politically correct term we have coined for the politically incorrect term batching bastard.

Okay, so I exaggerate, but really, it's similar to someone who just quit cigarettes. We all have a friend who has done this: once they quit they become a catalyst for others who smoke and lead them to "see the light." More importantly, those who truly kick the habit can't believe they smoked for all those years.

I'm sure some of you think I am crazy ... even my own father did! We used to argue about batching vs. flow every Thanksgiving (we had interesting family meals). Even though he had been introduced to the concepts and new technology way before his competition, he eventually went out of the cabinet-making business because his batching system could not compete with his competitors who adopted one-piece flow.

I think it is because of this, that I personally feel I must crusade against batching whenever and wherever I see it. When I am watching any manufacturing, service industry, health care, or government agency process, I cannot help but to see every lost part, upset customer, or patient waiting in a queue; lost process output and profitability; or our hard-earned tax dollars going down the drain whenever there is batching. Many who have worked with me on the shop floor have experienced me saying "Look! You just lost another piece there. Did you see it?" *But the real challenge is always getting everyone else to see it.* This is where the video camera* comes in handy.

As we said before, I honestly believe we are born thinking batching is the one best way. Our logic goes like this ...

If I am doing a process, which has multiple steps, and I start to work on the first step then I might as well complete the first step on the rest of them first and then go to the second step and so on until the batch (lot) of parts is completed.

Let's go back to our pen example. As long as I am putting the spring on one of the ink pens, why don't I do the same operation, i.e., put the springs on the rest of the pens first?

---

* The video camera is the greatest industrial engineering tool ever invented.

After all, isn't it more efficient that way? My brain tells me that it is. If I am going to hammer in some nails, "I might as well do them all at once so I don't have to put the hammer down each time and pick it up again." For the batchards out there, this is the point in the book where you are jumping up and down, screaming, "Finally, yes, I agree with this!" More importantly, if you didn't know you were a batchard and you found yourself exclaiming this ... then you are in fact a batchard ... but you are not alone, you have plenty of company (99% of the other people reading this book), and please know that there is still hope for you yet.

In my training classes, I ask the class, "How many of you are now convinced one-piece flow is better?" As we progress through the 5 days, each day I see more hands go up. At the end of the class the real honest people still don't raise their hands, and I know many of the people that do raise their hands may believe they truly "get it," but many really don't yet. It is just the way it is.*

Time and time again, look anywhere, on any line or in any transactional process and you see people batching. In Figure 8.2 we see a batching fixture. They exist all over companies that have a batching system. We pay well-meaning industrial engineers to design them. There is no reason these parts cannot be set up to be built one-piece flow. However, once we have this fixture in place we have now created and formalized the batching process and reinforced the batching mindset. It will now be even more difficult to implement one-piece flow once we give people the means to batch and feed their insatiable appetite for their batching paradigm.

Here's an everyday example: I ordered two fish sandwiches at a popular fast-food restaurant. What does the operator do? She grabs two bottom buns and sets them on the counter,

---

* Every one-piece flow/Lean practitioner goes through this with every company, having to start this batch to one-piece flow journey over and over again, always getting the same objections and questions. It comes with the territory. But if it weren't for this we wouldn't be in business ☺.

Figure 8.2 Batching fixture created by a well-meaning industrial engineer. (Source: BIG Archives.)

and then she gets two slices of cheese and puts one piece of cheese on each one. Then she gets two fish fillets and puts one on each bun, then she puts the special sauce on each fillet, followed by the top buns, and then she wraps each one up (see Figure 8.3). If the sandwiches are both for me, I get them at the same time. However, if someone else orders a fish sandwich right *after* me, then I end up waiting until his or her sandwich is done (along with mine) before I get *my* fish sandwich; this takes us back to Freddie's scenario.

A good analogy for batching is to imagine putting a taxi meter in place on your process. There are two sides to the taxi meter. One side calculates your fee based on the travel distance. This meter runs when you are moving and making progress (flowing) toward your destination. The second part of the meter starts counting whenever you stop (downtime clock). Whether it is for a red light or traffic congestion, this side of the meter goes to town. From the rider's point of view we really only want to be charged based on the run-time because this is the only real value-added time to us. The taxi

Figure 8.3 Fast-food sandwich-making: batch. (Note: It is not always batch but normally when order(s) are larger than one piece they batch. This is human nature.) (Source: BIG Archives.)

driver sees it differently; his value-added time is the entire time you are in the car. Imagine putting a taxi meter on *your* process … what percentage of the total time would consist of the run-time dollars vs. the wait-time dollars?

Many times it may be part of your organization's vision that drives batching (i.e., we've always done it this way, or we've done it this way for 34 years*), resulting in a natural cultural resistance to change. For example, a new CEO who knows nothing about one-piece flow can easily and even instantly kill all the progress the company has made with their one-piece flow program—sometimes without even knowing or realizing they are doing it. Sadly, we see this happen over and over again.

---

* Those of you who know me can hear me saying this somewhat dramatically in a very loud voice ☺.

One-piece flow is so hard to put in place because of the batching mindset; yet it is so easy to dismantle. As hard as it is to convert people to one-piece flow, it initially doesn't take long for them to go back to their comfort zone of batching. If it is not somehow truly interwoven into the culture, and supported with standard work and the drive for continuous improvement, complacency will set in, and one-piece flow will not sustain. Why? Because all of us are constantly trying to undo it with our minds!

Fact: Secretly, even those of us with the one-piece flow paradigm, deep down, still have a buried desire to batch. Do not underestimate the power of our minds.

Chapter 9

Light Shined on the Hidden Costs of Batching

Batching Is Bad!

This has been the basic concept throughout this book, but, now that we know the root causes ... what are the effects? What types of problems does batching really create?

Timeout 7

Before reading further, how many problems can you list that come with batching systems/processes (see Timeout 7)?

Our list includes the HIDDEN COSTS (see Table 9.1) and other impacts listed below

- QUALITY: Problems aren't found until the batch is completed, forcing the whole lot to be scrapped or reworked.

Timeout Exercise #7

- How many problems can you list that come with batching systems/processes?

I. _____

II. _____

III. _____

IV. _____

V. _____

VI. _____

VII. _____

VIII. _____

IX. _____

X. _____

Table 9.1   Result vs. Impact of Batching Production

Result	Impact
Labor was performed (potentially paid labor for working on something not needed) $$	→ Labor, material
Storage space required until it is needed $$	→ Expense
Expediting orders, creating a "hot list" and stopping work on one order to work on another $$	→ Labor, customer satisfaction
Product is wasted if it expires before it is ever needed or shipped (i.e., buffer solutions) $$	→ Labor, material, possible capital
Rework and scrap $$	→ Labor, material

Source: Updated from the Lean Practitioner's Field Book. Used with permission.

■ REWORK: Batching inevitably leads to rework. Since we normally don't inspect or test the batch until the end, when we find if one part is bad then they are usually all bad.

Fact: Once you build rework into the system, the motivation to fix the problem goes away.

■ Batching hides problems and discourages rework. Even though factories may keep track of scrap and rework, and yes, sometimes they launch a project to try to figure out the root cause, most of the time they don't figure it out, because in reality they don't have to. There is now plenty of inventory to cover up the problems. This means they build that rework into their system.

I was recently at a fast-food restaurant, and my son ordered two sides of eggs. We were told by the manager to pull up into the drive-through parking space and that it would be a couple minutes because they had to make a new batch of eggs. Ten minutes later, we received the two sides of eggs. Oddly enough, they had two drive-through parking spaces

Figure 9.1 Parking spots for drive-through customers. Next will there be a sign for parking space #4? (Source: BIG Archives.)

(see Figure 9.1). What does this mean for the people working the drive-through processes? It means now they have a place to put people when they can't get the order ready in time. Now I ask you … what drive-through customer wants a parking spot? However, once the parking spot is created there is no incentive to fix the problems. The pressure is off the team.

At one company they have conveyors that connect their machines so they can do one-piece flow. There is a continuous argument about these conveyors. The argument is: we should take out these conveyors because in reality we never use them. We always have problems and end up taking parts off the line and batching the parts. Can you predict what will surely happen if they remove the conveyors? They will NEVER fix the problems.

Management, instead of even tolerating their argument, should start fixing the problems so the parts can flow from one machine to the next, since one-piece flow is the goal!

∎ LONGER LEAD TIMES: The more batching, the more inventory, which further delays shipping our product or service to the customer and results in longer lead times. Because our lead times are longer, our customers must forecast for longer periods and sometimes order more than they need or before they need it. If a competitor then approaches your customer with a shorter lead time and comparable price, where will they go?

∎ SPACE: Batching creates the need for more space, which is driven by the entire stored inventory collected during, and between, processes. Layouts are the biggest driver of the eight wastes. Batching drives layouts!

∎ STORAGE: Yes, more space is required with batching, but where are those batches stored? Racks, shelves, tables, etc. are all needed in greater numbers to store inventory and hence greater capital spend.

∎ TRANSPORTATION: This is another one of the eight wastes that grows linearly with batching; again, because it forces space and storage in the layout.

I recall early in my career, we committed to attempting one-piece flow at a heat exchanger company that had about $45 million in sales. After a few years on the journey, we had a moment of clarity … we realized the number of forklift trucks employed in the plant had dropped from eight to three. During this time our sales increased to $72 million. We also found our net assets employed were decreasing thereby increasing our return on investment; maintenance was less, and more capital was available for growth vs. high inventory and transportation costs. Concurrently, we realized we had taken down more than 20 inventory racks, freeing up much-needed space. We actually traded the excess inventory racks for shipping credit with a local transportation trucking company.

∎ TRACKING INFORMATION: Batching forces us to create cost accounting standards, labor collection processes, and tools to track the "standard" cost of the batches as they move through the factory. We end up searching through that entire inventory and WIP in order to find the next order, or an order a customer is screaming for us to ship. It is not unusual to find manufacturing and materials employees in "hour(s)-long" production status meetings.

■ RESOURCES: Batching ties up more materials, space, and people resources, which results in more production and inventory and control people to schedule, expedite, and track the product as it moves through the factory. Tom Peters once said in his video, entitled *Speed is Life*, while referring to then president Von Beals at Harley Davidson, "We used to have 27 production controllers and nothing ever went out on time. Now we have one production controller and everything goes out on time."*

■ LACK OF RESPECT FOR PEOPLE: Batching leads to repetitive motion problems and requires sit-down operations that result in increased health issues. Batching in essence turns people into robots.

■ POOR DELIVERY: Batching slows down product velocity and throughput time, resulting in longer lead times and repair times for our customers.

■ CUSTOMER SATISFACTION: Batching results in poor customer satisfaction due to missed schedules, with 80% to 90% on-time delivery to customer promised dates (if they even measure it) and less to customer request date.

■ EXCESS and OBSOLETE INVENTORY: Invariably, batching results in greater amounts of excess and obsolete (E&O) inventory write offs. This could be due to engineering changes, damage during transportation, exceeding shelf life, and oxidation.

In the case of a company turnaround we are currently engaged in, we had a change in management philosophy

---

* *Speed is Life*, Tom Peters, a co-production of Video Publishing House and KERA, 1991.

from the prior owner's tenure. After taking over direction of the company, several years back, the son decided to outsource more subassemblies, which previously were in-house manufactured subcomponents made in a batch environment. A couple of years ago, we purchased the business and quickly became frustrated because every time we wanted to get at some usable part, we had to move several pallets, boxes, skids, etc. of these subcomponent materials. When we would inquire with one of our employees, who was a real concrete-head, as to what was on the skid or in the wooden box, the response frequently sounded something like this:

- Employee: "Oh, those are mostly good parts that we might use sometime. We don't want to throw those away."
- Owner: "Can we use them right now?"
- Employee: "It is a subcomponent to a subassembly that we now purchase."
- Owner: "Before I look at the bill of material [BOM*] and routers, would you like to tell me your opinion on whether or not we would ever be making this part in-house again or using it or setup the parts."
- Employee: "It would not make sense. We no longer have the machine to do the complete assembly and besides the whole assembly can be done for less outside."
- Owner: "Then why don't we throw them out so I don't have to @#$%^&* move them around one more time."
- Employee: "Well, those that aren't rusted are still good parts, it seems to be a real shame to throw them out."
- Owner: "What is a shame is that we continue to spend the company's money moving what you have now acknowledged are totally obsolete parts, back and forth, over and over again. I am happy to keep moving

---

* BOM is a list of parts required to make an assembly or product.

it around so long as we count the time against your vacation time."

– Employee: "Hmmm, Maybe we should throw them out then."

Since that conversation, we can comfortably say that three scrap metal dumpsters and 12 nonmetal dumpsters of "obsolete inventory and stuff" have been discarded in the last 18 months. Engineering changes, transportation damage, mice making nests in nonmetallic parts, oxidation, business model changes, market demand changes, etc. all lead to costly E&O write offs from our old batch environment. Batching is the silent killer of productivity!

■ CASH FLOW: Increasing inventories directly correlate to the cash we have tied up in "stored labor." Stored labor is labor we cannot use elsewhere, as it has already been expended working on the inventory we don't need. Cash is also represented in the material itself. Batching companies normally run three to four, and at most six to eight, inventory turns, tying up precious company cash. Batching leads to noncontinuous cash flows, as products are shipped and then invoiced in batches. This leads to cash shortages and additional financing costs. Prior to investigating, this excess inventory was silently bleeding the company of cash and destroying productivity.

■ PROCESS CHALLENGES: Many times going from batch to one-piece flow solves hidden manufacturing process challenges.

At one company we were seam-welding strips of metal into a circle. The company's batch processing method always presented problems getting perfectly concentric circles. Once we switched them to one-piece flow, they couldn't *help* but get perfect circles. By going to one-piece flow the metal was still hot from the welding machine and was easily shaped into the circle pattern. During the batch process, the parts sat around and waited prior to the flanging machine operation, and cooled. Once cooled, it was difficult to get the metal formed properly, and they were always a bit out of round.

A different company manufactured small delicate electronic gyros and had a 90% defect rate. We found out that, even though the parts were in a class 10,000 clean room, they were still exposed to the air and airborne contaminates for almost 6–8 weeks, which was how long it took to get through the entire process. By switching to one-piece flow we had the parts sealed within hours, thus reducing the opportunity to be contaminated. This increased the first pass yield to almost 100%, i.e., virtually zero defects.

■ INVENTORY: The byproduct of batching is inventory: the more batching, the more inventory produced. Batched inventory hides problems and drives overproduction. Waste of overproduction is evident whenever

  – We build more than we need, i.e., excess number of pieces,

    or

  – We build prior to when we need it.

Fact: Let's sum this section up by agreeing that batching is the major root cause of waste and drives overproduction. Now say it with me, ***"Batching is the silent productivity killer!"***

Timeout 8

Look at your personal batching list. What hidden costs exist? List them (see Timeout 8).

Wherever There Is Excess Inventory, a Problem Is Lurking

I was formerly in a purchasing role for a Fortune 50 aerospace company. We desperately needed parts for a military application to support Operation Desert Storm. We had ordered

Timeout Exercise #8

- Look back to your list from Timeout 5. Think about the hidden costs during these batching examples. What are some you can think of?

_____
_____
_____
_____
_____
_____
_____
_____
_____
_____
_____

- Estimate these expenses to the best of your knowledge. Seeing numbers on paper will help you comprehend the hidden amount.

_____
_____
_____
_____
_____
_____
_____
_____
_____
_____
_____

100 parts from a supplier, which were not due to be shipped for 6 more weeks. But obviously, in this case, we really couldn't wait the 6 weeks. In fact, they would most likely be delayed more than that anyway; there was no time to wait, we needed them right away. There are occasions when time is of the essence, and any delivery, even a small lot, is better than none at all and can at least get you started.

So I called the supplier and asked if he could speed up deliveries and was told, "The best we can do is three to four weeks, but no guarantees." I asked him to explain the *entire* manufacturing process to me and tell me where the parts were currently in the process. When he finished I found out they were manufacturing parts in lots of 50 pieces, and the first 50 pieces had just made it through the second of 10 operations. He said it would take least 3–4 weeks to get the first 50 pieces through the process, then the second batch of 50 were scheduled to be on time in 6 weeks. I told him I needed him to expedite them through the process. He told me that for a "substantial fee," he could get me the parts in 2 weeks. I told him that was still not acceptable. So, I then offered to buy all of their capacity for the 10 machine/operations for 2 days (24 hours a day if necessary) and told him I wanted him to set up these machines for our parts and hand-carry these parts through the factory, one-piece flow. I told him I wanted them shipped every time he got five parts completed, and send them by taxicab. He did, and we got our parts starting the next day, and completed the *entire* order within the 2 days.

Fact: One-piece flow reduces lead times from weeks or months to days or hours!

Are You Working on What You Really Need?

We have a saying with one-piece flow:

> *When you work on something you don't need,*
> *you can't work on something you do need!*

While this saying sounds simple, it is the premise underlying all overproduction. The problem is people violate it all the time. A common example of overproduction in manufacturing is building subassemblies offline, or pulling in shipments from next month, to this month, in order to make the revenue targets, or building 3 months' worth of parts at one time and then shipping them to the customer as needed. Whenever we build more than we need, or build it before it is needed, we are overproducing. It is the most difficult waste to overcome in any manufacturing organization because all of our results-focused metrics, and most of our MBA schooling, drive this waste of overproduction. All this material is produced *"just in case"* we need it, or in order to "make the numbers."

Think of the behaviors that this batching mindset drives. The practice of bringing in "batches" of product before they are needed requires more labor and space to handle all the extra demand in the system. We have to call the suppliers, rearrange their schedules, pay expediting charges, work overtime, and rush jobs through, creating scrap and rework, all to "make the end-of-the-month numbers." Batching production can result in the following, depending on what is being produced:

A product, piece of information, or person in a batch process spends most of its time (greater than 80%) in waiting (storage) and, typically, less than 1% in a value-added process. Inventory queues in the process result in longer throughput times, requiring more inventory, rooms, and staff and larger waiting rooms in order to fill the demand. This adds cost to the entire system and also creates unhappy customers. Batching doesn't really save us anything in the long run; it only costs us valuable time, space, and money.

Exercise: Walk through your shop. Look for the oldest work in process inventory and write down the date; do the same for finished goods and for raw material. What did you find? Did it match your computer system?

We worked with a company that made chemical detection equipment for the military. Prior to one-piece flow, it took almost eight operators to get one unit per day. After one-piece flow we cut the number to two operators, and eventually one operator could get two units per day by themselves. One-piece flow helped this company secure more contracts, increase their product offerings, and even expand into a new facility. *See Results section in the Appendix.*

Timeout 9

Pull out your batching list from above. Reflect on your list and see if you can think of any problems that arose from your or your company's batching behaviors. Save your list for later (see Timeout 9).

Errors and Defects

Now, let's explore defects and errors together. With one-piece flow we learned each step in a process is an opportunity for a defect. If we can eliminate the step in the process, we also eliminate the opportunity for the defect, thus improving quality. Batching creates boundless opportunities for errors; these errors ultimately turn into defects.

It is important here, I think, to explain the difference between an error and a defect. For instance, there is nothing worse than sour milk. The "error" is the expired milk in the fridge; the "defect" occurs when you drink it. It is important to note that errors don't always turn into defects. For instance, the milk might be expired but still ok to drink. So the date is to help expose and prevent the error so the defect doesn't occur. When we batch, there are many opportunities for errors to occur, but typically we don't find them until the entire batch is produced so they turn into defects.

Timeout Exercise #9

- Pull out your batching list again. Reflect on your list and see if you can think of any problems that arose from your or your company's batching behaviors. Save this list for later.

I. _____

II. _____

III. _____

IV. _____

V. _____

VI. _____

VII. _____

VIII. _____

IX. _____

X. _____

Since we don't normally find the defects until the end, when all of our cost is in the product (think back to our cookies), we end up having to rework the parts, adding yet more cost to the product. This impacts our internal and external quality rating and our ability to deliver on time. It could create the need to expedite the rework, or new lot of parts, thus forcing us to juggle customer deliveries, which ultimately affects the morale of our employees, makes us less profitable and less competitive, and threatens all of our jobs.

When One Is Bad They Are All Bad

This next company believed in mass "batch" production. Their best customer needed 1,000 parts right away, a large and significantly profitable order for the company. The president of the company and the president of the customer were good friends and often golfed together. This relationship put more pressure on the factory to get their parts out right away. Operations, knowing the importance of this VIP customer, put two full-time production control people on the order for 2 days to track, expedite, and report on the order's progress at each production step and make sure the parts never sat waiting before or after any operation. The parts were made in record time, and everyone up to that point was happy.

The last stop for the order was final test and inspection. Inspection found a tolerance stack-up issue on one of the subassemblies in the completed parts. It was determined that a washer within the subassembly did not meet the flatness specification. Somehow, the washer made it through incoming inspection, where flatness was a key characteristic for the part and should have been caught. The inspector who signed off the paperwork, of course, insisted he performed the check. So the hunt went on to try to find someone to blame when the report had to be made back to the president.

At this point, because they batched everything, each completed part in the lot had to be disassembled in order to retrieve the subassembly and then the subassembly reworked to replace the bad washer. However, they soon realized that every other subassembly waiting in the stockroom had the incorrect washer as well. Since they had prebuilt (again batched) and stocked all the subassemblies, they were not sure if they had all bad washers or not, so they had to go through and 100% inspect all the subassemblies to see if they contained the bad washer. After 100% inspection, they didn't find one part that met the spec. The next step was checking all the washers left in stock … they were bad as well. It turns out the supplier also batched all their parts! Since there was no way they could recover in time, the manufacturing manager had to explain to the president what happened. The president was furious and told the manufacturing manager "heads will roll over this!" The manufacturing manager proceeded to fire the inspector, and that weekend the president ended up playing golf without a complete foursome.

Fact: Finding and assigning blame never solves the problem … it just gets in the way of finding the real root cause.

Batching Means Lost Opportunities

At another company we were building rather large products for the construction industry. One day, after we had set up their new one-piece flow line, I overheard a conversation in the sales department. A customer had called and was desperate for one of their units. They were willing to pay a significant expediting fee (30% more of the price quote) if we could ship them a unit right away. Does this sound familiar to my previous scenario? Well, simply put, we are talking about thousands of dollars of additional profit; yet, because the production schedule was full, they turned the customer, along with their extra money, away.

Meanwhile, after implementation of one-piece flow, the company could now build six units per day, where it used to take 6 weeks. We found out later that the units we built during the time the customer needed them so badly were put on credit hold and could not ship! As it turns out, credit hold was a way for the sales people to get their units built early. In the past this guaranteed they would have them when their customer wanted them. All of a sudden, since the new line was installed, they now had this new "problem," which was that they could build these units right away. There was no longer a need for this "credit hold" strategy. Sales just needed to tell us the "real" date in the future.

Regardless, this meant that all the units we were building would end up in a storage area, sometimes for days, but normally weeks, just waiting to ship. So all this time we were producing units we did not need, when we could have satisfied a desperate customer and made quite a bit of extra money in the process.

One other problem the company found was that sales typically told customers they had a couple weeks after the order was placed to make changes. However, since we could now build them right away using one-piece flow, we were receiving change notices "after they were already built." We had to retrain the sales people, which was no easy task. All sales people like to "pad" their delivery schedules in the factory.

One thing you should notice is that while the term "effect" is not connotatively a negative word, there was not a single positive effect that batching produces listed in this chapter. The reason behind this is we haven't found any. We have learned what can cause batching, and now we have learned some of the impacts batching can have on a system. Next we will look at the concept of batch and waste. Really a lot of it comes down to one question ...

Chapter 10

Which Came First, Batching or the Eight Wastes?

Batching Is the Root Cause of the Eight Wastes*

Most of you reading this book have probably heard of the eight wastes. We believe the root cause of these eight wastes can, almost every time, be traced back to batching, inherent somewhere in the process. Let's review each waste:

1. **Overproduction**

   Overproduction is the number one worst waste. We have discussed several examples already of how batching, in its very nature, drives overproduction. It is just a normal byproduct of the batching system.

2. **Overprocessing**

   Batching drives much of the waste of overprocessing. Normally, there is a lack of standard work when it comes to batch processes. There may be work instructions, but

---

* The eight wastes are derived from the Toyota Production System and credited to Taiichi Ohno.

143

these are not quite the same as standard work. Standard work means we do it exactly the same way, every time, with a standard amount of inventory, and within about the same amount of time. But with batching, we find every operator does it a different way.

To explain further, at one company, I witnessed a process where operators were taking small steel-plated parts and lining them up on trays. All three operators performed a "batch process"; however, each batched the process *differently*. Operator #1 would stack all the parts up and then lay them out on the tray, Operator #2 would take them as they were and lay them out on the tray, and Operator #3 would grab parts in bunches, however many he could fit in one hand, and lay them out. While the result is a tray lined with parts, there was a significant variation in the times it took for each tray to be completed when measured between operators.

3. Transportation

Whenever we hear the word "transport" applied to moving product, we subconsciously hear the words "by batching" right after it. If my machine is 12 feet or 3.6 meters away from the next machine, I am not going to do one-piece flow, end of story. To do one-piece flow, one must put all machines and processes as close together as physically possible, or it will not succeed.

4. Waiting or Idle Time

Waiting is also a root cause of batching. As discussed earlier, when someone is idle they will find a way to batch. This not only wastes labor time, because the person is now overproducing, but they are also now working on something we don't need, instead of something we do need. The worst part is that in the employee's mind, they are helping, or doing something positive, and most managers would walk by and be pleased. What you can't possibly realize just walking through your company is that the busiest people are not always the most efficient.

These busybodies could be creating more work for the next step in the process and, silently, could be derailing productivity.

Most idle time is driven by layouts and "*isolated islands.*" Isolated islands are work areas where the operator is literally stuck and can't flex to another workstation or bump another operator. This results in fractional labor and is very inefficient and costly. Imagine a factory that measures the amount of worker idle time; imagine the surprised look on supervisors' faces walking through the plant. We see this same waste in offices as well; the idle time in any office would surprise everyone, even the people working in it. Batching drives the development of these wasteful layouts.

Typically, whenever we hear the words we're going to "centralize," it really means, "we're batching!" Companies will sometimes spend thousands, sometimes even millions, of dollars switching from decentralized to centralized offices, departments, manufacturing centers (i.e., supplying multiple plants), call centers, or other types of layouts. They see a quick improvement on the graphs because they laid off people when they bunched the procedures in one area, but then they will typically experience problems less than a year into the process when they realize the one department can't meet customer demand. They then decide to add more employees to the system, and when that doesn't work, it's back to decentralizing. The biggest issue is that companies don't position departments correctly. They'll have a large separated office for the Accounts Payable team, and the Sales team will be positioned on the other side of the building. Why not make accounts payable part of Purchasing and accounts receivable part of Sales? Wouldn't that make more sense? Akio Yamada writes in his book called *The Happiest Company*, edited by Norman Bodek, about Mirai Industry, which has the highest employee satisfaction rate in Japan.

Mirai has never lost any money since its inception, every year for 50 years. Every employee is empowered to make decisions that affect their work without asking their boss or discussing with fellow employees—true self-reliance. Mirai doesn't even have accounting or HR departments because both are considered non-value added. They have the longest paid vacation and shortest working hours in Japan; everyone is full time; there is no overtime, no sales quotas, and they do not measure people's performance. Every five years all 850 employees go on an overseas trip. You get paid $6.00 for every mistake you make and you are encouraged to make mistakes and learn from them, but don't repeat them. There is no carrot and stick. If you fail, the supervisor will say "Good job"—no scolding—at least you tried. Managers are prohibited from giving orders to subordinates—people are treated with respect. As a result, they get around 10,000 implemented ideas per year and have 90% of the market share in switchboxes; and Mirai was in the top 20 companies in Japan for obtaining new patents, and they aren't the cheapest.

5. Inventory

Excess inventory is the direct result of batching. It ties up precious cash and much-needed space and spawns defects. Inventory is evil like all the books say, but batching drives the inventory. It is the root cause, so in reality, logic dictates it is really batching that is the root of all evil!

6. Excess Motion

Excess motion, like idle time, comes from poor workstation design or poor layouts. Workstations and layouts designed in batch environments always require excess motion for the operators and normally have major ergonomic issues. Workers are reaching, leaving their stations to search for things, bending over to get something from the batch of parts on the floor, waiting, or bending over to put a part on top of the pile of the next batch. When we have to move more, we try to do "too much" in each step, so as to not have to do the movement over again. Have you ever reached into the washing machine and grabbed one item at a time? If you're like everyone else you reach in and grab as much as you can at once to then throw it into the dryer. I fall victim as well, but guess how many times I have dropped an item onto the floor, caught a loose string that rips, or worse, tossed an item my wife told me "not to dry" into the dryer because it was lost in the heap of clothes in my arms. If I did it one-piece flow, I would avoid a lot of arguments when, all of a sudden, certain articles of clothing no longer fit my spouse.

At one company they moved very heavy parts on trolleys. The trolleys were large and, when filled, it sometimes took two or three people to move them. Of course the employees would first try to move them by themselves. This resulted in many back injuries. We tried putting water levels on each trolley—a line of tape halfway down on the trolley—but the operators ignored it and kept filling them up. Finally we cut the trolleys in half so they would not hurt themselves.

7. Defects

Plain and simple, batching drives errors, which result in defects. One-piece flow systems in conjunction with successive checks will catch errors right away, thus minimizing the risk of defects in the balance of the parts to be produced. If the one-piece flow line has "mistake-proofing fixtures," then the number of defects will be much lower than batching. With one-piece flow, no parts are prebuilt and stocked as subassemblies; we don't have that problem of having to go back and 100% recheck all existing stock etc. or do any of the rework required that comes with batch systems.

8. Talent

The last waste is the waste of talent, or not utilizing people to their fullest potential. Batching systems turn people into robots. Employees do the same small job, over and over and over again. As a result, batching is a primary cause of repetitive motion injuries, that is, strained muscles, injured backs, carpal tunnel, etc.

With one-piece flow, the operators work across multiple workstations, and their motions change from station to station. In addition, workers cross-train and learn new skills. Morale is better. Workers stand and walk, getting exercise vs. sitting all day with the potential for gaining weight and creating health problems. They are continuously thinking about how to improve processes and make it easier while maintaining or improving quality. One-piece flow supports the respect for humanity principle, and people go home feeling like winners knowing they accomplished something, as opposed to reworking parts all day.

Little's Law

Little's Law* quantifies the effects of batching and queuing. The more batching that exists in our system, the longer it takes to get the product through the system, i.e., "throughput time." If we divide throughput time (the total time in the process) by the cycle time—how often we get a piece out of the process—it will tell us exactly how much inventory—WIP—is in our system. The more batching that goes on, the more WIP that is in our system, and the more problems are magnified throughout the supply chain. This magnification of inventory and communication problems becomes very evident in a simulation we use, called the Beer Game.†

Batching systems by their very nature are not level-loaded. This creates variation in demand cycles. When demand is up, we end up working overtime. When demand decreases, we send people home. The more we batch the longer our

---

* Little's Law states that the quantity of pieces WIP (Work in Process Inventory) = Throughput Time/Cycle Time.

† The Beer Game was developed by Jay Forrester, professor emeritus at MIT during the1960s.

delivery times (Little's Law), the less flexible we become to our customers. Let's say our lead time is 8 weeks because we are batching. This causes our customers to have to forecast their demand for 2 months. We all know a good forecast is an oxymoron. So, chances are what we are building for them is not going to be what they need, hence we are working on products we don't need when we should be working on products our customers DO need.

If we can do one-piece flow and reduce our lead time to 1 week or less, then our customer only has to forecast 1 week out, and now we can start to look at vendor-managed inventory—VMI* systems, or kanban—with our customers and with our suppliers.

The Easy Way Out

Whenever you find yourself thinking "it would be a lot easier if we did it this way," check to make sure it is not a batching solution.

One small company we worked with was a custom gear manufacturer and, being a small business, cash flow was extremely important. They had a 6-month backlog of orders and, literally, a wall of parts that were just started or semi-finished, but all required either a complicated setup or some obstacle to getting it completed. The closer they got to the end of the month, the more pressure there was to find the easiest thing they could work on and get out the door. Therefore, the schedule meant nothing. It came down to, "What parts we can batch through the fastest?" Some of the parts on this wall were over 2 or 3 years old, and the customers were still expecting the parts!

Fact: This situation is inherent in any batching company. When a pile of orders are waiting, as humans, we are always

---

* VMI is a streamlined approach to inventory management and involves collaboration between suppliers and their customers where the suppliers manage the customer's inventory, and the customer is not charged until they use the inventory.

going to work on the easiest ones first, leaving the harder tasks for later or for others to work on. This is known to many by the term "cherry-picking."

Many large companies suffer this same syndrome, especially at the "end-of-the-month" crunch. They will sometimes pull in orders from one to 3 months out, if they have the parts and they are "easy" to get out. However, these wreak havoc with their internal systems, their supply chain and introduce chaos into the system. This havoc is never measured by their internal reports or financial systems. Therefore, they don't realize or even understand the chaos they are creating.

This phenomenon has resulted in supply chain managers losing their jobs, or suppliers losing business, because of the way the material requirements planning system "jerks" them around. In reality, it is management's fault because they are creating this system in order to "make the numbers." Ask anyone who has experience with "materials management," and they will vouch for this syndrome.

The one-piece flow solution is to level-load the work as much as possible based on the actual customer requested date and to avoid offering quantity discounts. This eliminates large fluctuations in demand in the factory and makes scheduling manpower and capacity planning much easier. However, this requires a huge leap of faith for most companies, because none of the hidden costs associated with pulling in orders or working on the easiest ones first are exposed by traditional accounting systems.

We've all been in this scenario; management asks you to carry out an order that you know will come back and haunt you in the future, and you can't tell them "I told you so" and expect to have a job. Now what you *can* do is explain to them, using the eight wastes along with the eight root causes of batching, as to why their task may be flawed, and how batching will really set you back further than if you weren't to complete the task. Tread carefully—we're not telling you to go in "arms waving"—but if you find you have trouble conveying it to management, feel free to give us a call.

Chapter 11

Debunking the Myths

Batching Myths

Myth: Batching Is Quicker than One-Piece Flow

Here we must present two stories:

A friend of mine, to whom this book is dedicated, was very interested in one-piece flow but just could not wrap his arms around the concept. He had instructed his workers to do five-piece batches (see Figure 11.1) because he was convinced that was the most efficient way. Interestingly, he did not want to do larger batches because, in his mind, anything larger than five pieces was less efficient. To this day I am not sure where the number five came from.

In order to prove one-piece flow was more efficient, we conducted a trial using his way vs. my way so I agreed I would film the current process. While I was videoing each trial it was so obvious to me that one-piece flow was more efficient. However, it was not obvious to him. We all take in and process information differently. So in reality there is no such thing as common sense. Each of our "common senses" is different.

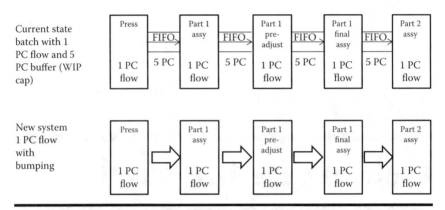

Figure 11.1 One-piece flow with five-piece buffer (WIP cap) compared to one-piece flow with bumping. Even though there are FIFO lanes in the top example, they were losing FIFO due to batching. In addition, it was not unusual to do more than five at a time. (Source: BIG Archives.)

Prior to this trial I had presented every argument I could think of as to why batching was bad and one-piece flow was better. We then witnessed many of these, and some new ones, during the batch video trial.

During the trial we saw clutter and materials everywhere. On the first step the operator did more than the five pieces, because he lost count. After the first production step, the parts were supposed to go into a basket to go to the washer. However, the operator did not follow the procedure and moved them onto the next table instead of the basket for the washer. The second operator came over and started using the nonwashed parts (which now just became defects). I let these parts continue until just prior to final assembly to show the problems with batching. They ended up with 10 pieces that had to be completely disassembled and then washed and then re-assembled. This is typical of batch production. However, my friend felt this was a normal problem in production and could happen any time, so it did not persuade him. I tried emphasizing the need for standard work and pointed out that one-piece flow would

- Produce higher output
- Reduce his backlog
- Improve quality (parts that did not get washed)
- Make the area easier to manage
- Reduce his WIP alone—in his mind it didn't matter because the RM inventory is already there
- Speed up his velocity, i.e., the throughput time

None of these arguments worked. Finally, as we were taking cycle times, my friend said, "Ok, give me the cycle time for doing this assembly operation (the second station) for batching." So as he requested we took the split time for each operation. I argued this was not the correct way to measure the time because it did not take into account all of the waste in the batching system. This means you can't compare the assembly of individual parts to one-piece flow because it will take the same amount of time. You have to take the total time to do the five pieces and divide it by five to get the real cycle time. My friend said no, that this is what he wanted to do.

Once we finished that step, we looked at the one-piece flow trial video. The result of the trial was that the cycle time for one-piece flow was 40% faster than the overall batch cycle time. But this did not convince him either. So we watched the assembly on station two for one-piece flow and captured the time for each individual step. When my friend saw that the assembly time for each individual component in one-piece flow was the same as batch he finally said, in that jaw-dropping, pants-down moment: "OK, I get it now. I believe one-piece flow is the way to go." So what convinced him to "get it" was not all the waste in the batch process, the defects we incurred, or the longer overall cycle time. It was simply that the assembly times for each individual step were the same. The next day I asked him what convinced him flow was better, and he stated that in the end four things changed his mind.

■ Bottom line—he was convinced initially that batching was more efficient. The fact that the data showed the times for batching were not faster than one-piece flow is what he said convinced him. If only I had known this ahead of time.

■ He knew OPF was faster and the WIP and cycle time would be reduced. But he still thought the five-piece batch (no more than that) would work better to cover any variation in the process (note: variation forces us to batch!).

■ He felt operators would slow down if they don't see they have a buffer of five pieces but they didn't slow down when doing one-piece flow on the video.

■ Forces the team leader to stay on the line and make sure discipline is in place to follow the new process but with one-piece flow the team leader's job became easier to manage the line because there was not so much clutter.

I returned to the factory two months later, and guess what? They were still batching five pieces. I asked the plant manager why? He said he still wasn't convinced one-piece flow was better. Hmmm. I guess he really didn't "get it" after all. I am still working on him and know he will eventually come around, just not sure when.

The second case study was another friend of mine, now president of a large company, who was convinced that for his product line, which was grinding and finishing castings, two-piece flow with a two-piece buffer was the way to go. He had studied the process and was convinced this was the best way. It took me over four years to change his mind. Once again, he believed anything with more than two-piece flow was not efficient, and again I don't know where the magic number of two comes from. His logic was that there was so much variation in the product (variation forces you to batch) and finishing times that the two pieces they were working on would balance each other out, and if they

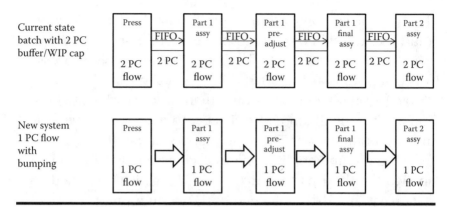

Figure 11.2 VSM one-piece flow vs. two-piece flow with two-piece buffer. (Source: BIG Archives.)

didn't, there was a two-piece buffer between each station to pick up the slack (see Figure 11.2). Finally, his production manager, on his own volition, tried one-piece flow and videoed it. He was amazed that it was actually faster and couldn't wait to tell his boss. He was so excited he interrupted our meeting to show us the video. His enthusiasm coupled with the video finally convinced the president to change his mind. Eventually we introduced bumping and achieved 40% to 60% improvements over the two-piece, two-buffer approach.

You just never know what is going to convince people to "get it," but normally videos become very useful in demonstrating the power of one-piece flow. *Seeing is believing* with many folks I deal with, and once they see it can be done, we experience that jaw-dropping moment that finally tells me, "They get it."

The One Time When Batching Is Actually Faster than One-Piece Flow

I know, the header says it all; how defeated I felt when I found that one time where batching was, in fact, faster than one-piece flow. It took over 25 years before I found it, and I found it while trying to prove to someone, on video, that one-piece flow would be faster. The assembly process was composed of three parts. The operator would lay out 25 pieces on a table. She would then pick up a Loctite bottle and apply a small amount of Loctite to each one, never setting the bottle down. Then she grabbed a handful of parts from the bin and applied one to each assembly. She then applied the third part to each of the 25, which remained stationary, and then tightened each one in a press. To my dismay, only one of my one-piece flow trials matched her cycle time.

Knowing batching couldn't really be the answer, I had to research and study this further. The reason for her speed in the batch process was the operator never picked up the parts and put them down. If you notice in our pen example in Chapter 5, each time the operator picked up all the parts and then put them down. Whenever I see this, I know one-piece flow can beat it. But when the parts never move, the time is normally close to one-piece flow. However, you still have a problem because you can't batch in the middle of a one-piece flow line, and you still have problems with defects in batching that don't get caught until the end of the process. So I determined that where one-piece flow had problems in this example was when the operator had to pick up and put down the Loctite bottle each time. Thinking creatively, and being fueled by the impossibility of batching even possibly being a little bit better than one-piece flow, we modified the one-piece flow process to have the Loctite bottle placed on a fixture with a foot pedal. Now that the system was one-piece flow, and we had removed the need to pick up the Loctite bottle, we beat the batching process "hands down." What this taught me was, even in a scenario where you tell yourself, "We've tried one-piece flow, but our batching is faster," there is a way one-piece flow can beat it.

Myth: One-Piece Flow Will Make Us Robots!

One of the big arguments we always hear is one-piece flow will make us robots. We have all heard this argument before.

But, in fact, one-piece flow and following standard work does not make us robots, and surely no more than batching does! If you go out and video any batching operation, where the operator repeats the same robotic task over and over again, sometimes for hundreds or thousands of pieces, you will see that batching is what really makes us robots. The operator never has to think. They go to the next step time and again and repeat the same step over and over. I have come to think that people really like feeling safe or just feeling comfortable with this ongoing repetitiveness, considering our innate need to batch. In general, most people don't like change.

One-piece flow lets you do several operations to a part (or administrative process) so that each part is completed at the end of a cycle. We also find out if the parts are good right away so we don't have to do rework. We then encourage the operators to start thinking about how to improve the operation as they go. We find most operators hate one-piece flow in the beginning but eventually grow to like it much better than batching.

When we visit companies a year later to follow up we find most operators never want to go back to the old batching environment. Post one-piece flow implementation, everything is organized, with everything where they need it; they like their jobs are better; and they have virtually no rework and feel like they are getting something accomplished each day.

Myth: Centralizing Is Better

Centralizing, as we said earlier, is a synonym for batching. As soon as we centralize something, we have to schedule it and then create processes for working within and around the process, department, or system. Some examples of centralizing are

- Instead of having a printer at each desk we have a centralized printer for the department.
- Removing registration from each department and creating a central registration group for the entire hospital.
- Instead of having each person responsible for customer service we create a customer service department.
- Accounting, purchasing, and other overhead type departments are typically centralized.
- Circuit City used this concept. When you purchased an item the sales person would write you up and then send you to a centralized area to pick it up. Once you got to this area, you had to wait sometimes quite a long time to get your item or find out it wasn't available. Of course Circuit City is no longer in business, although this may not be the reason why.
- The *centers of excellence* (basically creating a monopoly at one site) concept, where one plant does an entire product line for every other plant in the division or company, is another form of batching on a large scale.

The driver behind this thinking can always be traced back to the concept of economies of scale and the thought process that centralizing will make it cheaper and easier to manage.

However, consider the example we recently encountered in a hospital emergency department (ED). We needed a transport person to move a patient to the floor. We noticed a transport person right outside the ER. When we asked that person, who wasn't busy, if he could transport the patient, he told us we had to call the transport department. When we contacted the transport department they told us we could not use that person but had to wait for the next available person, who didn't arrive until more than 20 minutes later. Interestingly the transport department measured themselves on how fast they were able to answer people's calls and assign a person to the request, not on the length of time it took for a transporter to arrive once requested. When we implemented our flow-based solutions in hospitals we assigned transporters to surgery and the ED and cross-trained them so they could do other required tasks when not transporting, thus they were never idle but were now part of that department's budget. This gave each department total control over their process (destiny) and left no excuses for not transporting a patient in a timely manner.

Another way to think about it is the example of the printer above. IT will buy one very large printer, with bells and whistles people don't need for the department. They have to buy a big one because it is servicing so many people. But IT's thinking is that it is easier and cheaper for the IT department because they only have to buy and manage one printer vs. managing each person having their own smaller cheaper printer; but, they never consider the effect on the person doing the job. What is easiest for them? No one looks at the hidden costs behind each person losing time to go to the printer to get their report or printout. Many times, customers end up waiting while the person goes to the printer, which sometimes can be found quite a distance away. In addition, if there is a problem with the printer, instead of the person in the department being able to fix it they have to call the help desk. Ironically, the IT help desk is also a centralized area.

Now to be fair, being centralized isn't *always* bad. For instance, centralizing payroll makes total sense, but it is completely electronic. With flow thinking, we normally move companies toward decentralizing processes.

Batching Is a Hard Habit to Break

Our experience is that batching is so engrained in all of our minds it is a very difficult habit to break. Based on research, it is generally accepted that, on average, it takes up to 66 days

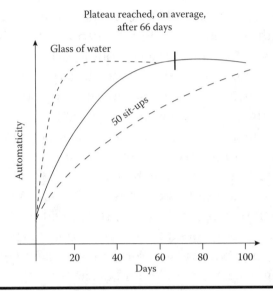

Figure 11.3   How long to form a habit. (Source: http://www.spring. org.uk/2009/09/how-long-to-form-a-habit.php, also Making Habits, Breaking Habits, Jeremy Dean, 0738215983-DeanFinal_Design 10/15/12 8:46 PM Page 6. Used with permission.)

to form a new habit and sometimes as many as 254 days to break a habit* (see Figure 11.3).

The good news is we can choose to change our batching behavior, but we have to have a compelling need to change in

---

* Jeremy Dean is the author of Psyblog and Making Habits, Breaking Habits, http://www.spring.org.uk/2009/09/how-long-to-form-a-habit.php. When the researchers examined the different habits, many of the participants showed a curved relationship between practice and automaticity of the depicted (solid line) (Figure 11.3). On average a plateau in automaticity was reached after 66 days. In other words, it had become as much of a habit as it was going to become. This graph shows early practice was rewarded with greater increases in automaticity, and gains tailed off as participants reached their maximum automaticity for that behavior. Although the average was 66 days, there was marked variation in how long habits took to form, anywhere from 18 days up to 254 days in the habits this study. As you'd imagine, drinking a daily glass of water became automatic very quickly, but doing 50 sit-ups before breakfast required more dedication (above, dotted lines). The researchers also noted that missing a single day did not reduce the chance of forming a habit. A subgroup took much longer than the others to form their habits, perhaps suggesting some people are "habit-resistant." Other types of habits may well take much longer.

order for this to happen and truly overcome the habit. Simply being dissatisfied or complaining about the process doesn't necessarily supply the compelling need to change. There are those people, and we all know who they are, who love to complain all day. I liken them to the ever-gloomy character Eeyore* in Winnie the Pooh or Debbie Downer on *SNL*.[†] However, if we have a truly compelling need to change, we can move toward eliminating the barriers that are preventing us from establishing one-piece flow. The reason for writing this book is to help inspire you and create that compelling need to change.

Timeout 10

Pull out your batch list again. Look it over. How hard a habit would it be, for you or your companies, to break any of the examples on your list and do one-piece flow (see Timeout 10)?

"Batching Habit Story"[‡]

There were two separate groups of volunteers working at a women's shelter. The first group of six volunteers served food to the tables between noon and 1:00 p.m. and was always looking to improve their process. The first process was to plate the food in advance, place the plates under food warmers until the women arrived, and then serve the food. They wanted to plate early because the first influx of 50 people came in at noon. By batching ahead of time they thought it would be easier to meet the initial demand. As a result,

---

* http://winniethepooh.disney.com/eeyore in Winnie the Pooh–Disney.
[†] Debbie Downer was a character portrayed on Saturday Night Live–http://www. nbc.com/saturday-night-live.
[‡] Story from the *Lean Practitioner's Field Book*, Protzman, Kerpchar, Whiton, Lewandowski, Grounds, Stenberg © 2015.

Timeout Exercise #10

- Pull out your batch list again. Look it over. How hard a habit would it be for you or your company to break any of the examples on your list?

_____

_____

_____

_____

_____

_____

_____

_____

_____

_____

_____

_____

_____

_____

_____

_____

_____

sometimes the food did not fit properly under the warmers and became cold, was overcooked, or had to be reworked by adding extra gravy to heat it up; all because they started plating too early.

After they improved their process, the food was plated from a steam table, one-piece flow, and each plate was made as the woman entered the dining room. The volunteers and especially the women really liked the new system.

On Mondays, a second group of three older volunteers brought in fresh fruit to serve to the women. They began washing and cutting the fruit at about 12:30 p.m. Then, they placed all the cut-up fruit on one platter and wheeled it through the dining room to serve to each table.

One day, the trio arrived so late that the women in the dining room had already started to leave. The first group of volunteers suggested to the three older volunteers, all batchards, to bring out whatever was already cut up and washed so at least the remaining women could get some fruit.

The trio was obstinate and so set in their ways they insisted on cutting up all of their bananas and apples to finish their platter. By the time they finally came out to the dining room, only 12 of the 75 women were still there to enjoy the fruit. Instead of two of them serving the women what was already prepared, while one volunteer continued to cut up the remaining fruit, they insisted on finishing their "batch" of fruit, the way they had always done it. Not only did they miss out on serving more women that day, they were left with food that, once cut up, had to be thrown away because it would not even keep until the next meal! When you think about it, they could have even handed out the uncut bananas to the women. Batching habits are hard to break.

Chapter 12

Batching vs. One-Piece Flow

Batching in Factories or Offices

I have never walked into any factory (or office) and had to talk people *out* of doing one-piece flow. Why? Because they never are—they are always batching. Even once they agree to try one-piece flow, they will want to run small lots first, i.e., five-piece batches through their production line. Our single largest battle is figuring out how to convince people one-piece flow is more efficient than batching. Each person is different in what it takes to convince him or her to convert from batching to flow. Sometimes, we have to make the changes in small steps from large batches to small batches, then from small batches to smaller batches, and then to one piece at a time. It normally takes time to overcome the reasons they are batching in the first place.

One approach is simply to ask them ... what is it going to take to convince you one-piece flow is better than batching? Once you get their objection, then you have to figure out how to overcome their objection. Sometimes videoing the process as batching and then as one-piece flow will work, but you must get them to agree up front on the metrics that will be used to make the decision. I have conducted many time studies, only to find the person did not agree with my metrics, so, I have learned the metrics have to come from them, and they need to lead the study.

It is also important to look at the overall value stream and not just timing one step in the overall process. Remember, as discussed earlier, there are some assembly process steps where initially batching may beat one-piece flow; however, once improvements are put in place, one-piece flow will win.

Prebuilding and Outsourcing Are Forms of Batching!

During our one-piece flow training classes, the batching paradigm becomes extremely evident. We conduct, as part of the training, a one-piece flow exercise in which there is a discussion on acceptable improvement ideas. The number one idea/ suggestion for improvement is always "Can *we* build up the subassemblies ahead of time?"

Most people don't feel or consider building ahead (prebuilding) as batching. In fact, most prebuilding is due to idle time and the need to fill that time with working on something. It is interesting to see that participants don't understand "prebuilding" is batching.

The next question is, "Can we outsource it and have a supplier build them, and ship them in pre-built?" This question always seems to come so easily. But note: outsourcing takes *our* people's jobs "off the line." Can the supplier really do it better and at less cost than you can? If the process involves very specialized, expensive equipment the answer may be yes, but otherwise, it should be cheaper to build it in-house once you "get" the one-piece flow paradigm. As soon as you outsource the product, you lose control over delivery, and quality may suffer. "Without due diligence and appropriate controls, outsourcing, many times, ends up being much costlier than in-house manufacturing or service (especially once you have applied the one-piece flow tools), resulting in high defect rates, late deliveries, poor service and customer dissatisfaction."*

It's kind of interesting. I am a big fan of the TV show *Top Chef*®. Whenever one of their chefs decides to batch (not just prep) ahead and make the entire meal ahead of time so they can serve it the next day, they lose. In one episode, one chef cooked to order, fresh and hot, while the other served their batch food that ended up being soggy. The cooked-to-order chef always wins. In another episode, during Restaurant Wars, the chef, who was going to be in charge of the front of the house, prepared crepes the night before, but when it came time to serve them, the chefs did not know what to do with them and heated them up when they were supposed to be served cold. The batching chef went home! Batching always gets you in trouble, and when it comes to food you are almost always better off cooking to order. This applies to anyone from chefs on TV, to at-home cooks, to cooks in hospital nutritional services departments. As Chef Ramsay says in his show *Kitchen Nightmares*, you should never have a microwave in your restaurant kitchen.

Batching (Like One-Piece Flow) Is a System

With every system come advantages and disadvantages. This is known as "systems thinking." Systems thinking is a philosophy that looks at the world through the lens of systems. Through this lens, we find all of our processes (whether business or personal) make up the system within which we have to work/ live. With systems thinking come certain principles; some of these are

---

* Govindarajan Ramu, http://asq.org/quality-progress/2008/08/global-quality/in-the-know.html.

- Everything in a system is interconnected. Therefore changes to one process impact other processes.
- Behaviors witnessed in one part of the system (company) are imbedded in the rest of the system.
- In order to make changes you must change the system, not just a part of a process. But small changes to the system can make big improvements.
- We are all victims of the systems in which we work/live. This is why blame just gets in the way of fixing the real problems. W. Edwards Deming said that 95% of the time it is the system that is to blame, not the person in the system.

Companies that batch share the same systemic problems with other companies that batch, because they are part of the batch SYSTEM. When we assess a batching company, we can normally predict where they are having problems (i.e., poor delivery, cash flow issues, two to three sigma, 95% to 99% quality, expediting, etc.). The senior leadership generally become very high-paid expediters in batch systems, and are always trying to make the end-of-the-month numbers. This is difficult, because they are always pulling orders in early from future months, causing more and more chaos in production. In these systems, they are always looking for someone to blame when there is a problem. Often adding inspection becomes the answer to fixing the problems. However, adding inspection, by itself, is never a good corrective action and should never be the only corrective action when a problem is found.

Once you initially create one-piece flow in an area, and reduce or eliminate batching, the following will occur:

- Floor space is reduced.
- Productivity increases, overtime hours decrease, and eventually overhead labor is reduced.
- Team members become very visible on the line, as there is now nowhere to hide, leading to more efficient (and easier) supervision of the one-piece flow lines.

- Supervisors have additional time to encourage ideas, cross-train employees, and work on improvements.
- There is a paradigm shift from a reactive to a proactive management approach.
- Problems and process or product variations become much more visually apparent.
- Results can occur quickly within a specific area or process.
- Root cause analysis solves the problems, which do not return unless a one-piece flow rule is violated.
- Market competitiveness increases with shorter lead times.
- Inventory turns increase.
- Storage areas are freed up, and less transportation of material will actually be noticed through the plant.

In many cases, even though we think we know, we really don't have a good understanding of what it means to batch paper processes or parts. A key part of our one-piece flow fundamentals training is to better understand what constitutes batching, why we batch, and why we think batching is better. See results section in Appendix.*

How Do You Sustain One-Piece Flow?

The only way to implement and sustain one-piece flow is with standard work, workplace organization (5S), setup reduction (SMED), and ultimately, preventative and predictive maintenance. In short, to help sustain one-piece flow, variation needs to be eliminated wherever possible (see Figure 12.1). We find most people underestimate the value and need for standard work and that many implementations fail over time because the standard work was on someone's computer who left the organization. Thus, it was never "built" into their system.

---

* Note: The results in the Appendix represent a small sample of our results. We have hundreds of great results across most industries.

Operator standard work form

Unit/Product/Service	Lunch	No. people needed	Total labor time:	Available time	Daily demand	Head count:	1	2	3	4	5
Tray line	Operator #3	2.351	21.00	7,200	806.000	Cycle time:	21	11	7	5	4
						Hourly output:	171	343	514	686	857
						Daily output:	343	686	1,029	1,371	1,714

Standard work area:

Job step #	Operation description	Time	Accum time
1	Pick up tray and place on counter	2	2
2	Pick up order ticket and read	2	4
3	Place order ticket in right hand corner of tray	1	5
4	Place product on top of order ticket	2	7
5	Place food onto tray per ticket	5	12
6	Pick up tray cover and place over tray	3	15
7	Place silverware/plasticware onto tray	2	17
8	Pick up tray and place into Aladdin cart	4	21

Layout area and walk patterns

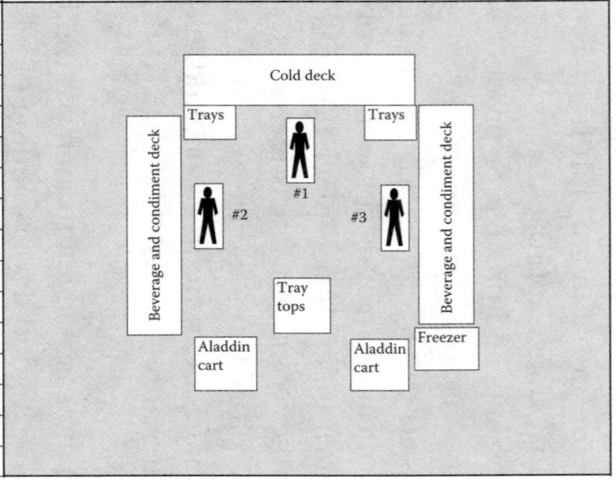

Figure 12.1 Standard work example. (From BIG Archives.)

Without Standard Work

- Everyone does the job a different way.
- If we eliminate a step in the process, that step will be in a different order for each operator, and for some operators it may not even exist.
- We lose predictability.
- We are dependent on those with the domain knowledge.
- We have poor quality. You cannot have quality without a standard.
- Batching returns!

With Standard Work We Can Sustain It

- Standard work is the vehicle we use to capture all of our improvements.
- We can use it along with our videos to train new employees.
- It is the block foundation of the learning organization (see Figure 12.2).
- We are no longer dependent on the workers who try to hoard their knowledge in order to keep their jobs and extort the company.
- If the manager leaves, we won't lose the system.
- If we eliminate a step, everyone across every shift eliminates the same step.

Fact: Standard work is the heart of the company. Without it, the company will never be as successful as it could be. The only way to really sustain is to build standard work into the very fabric of the organization. This means we must integrate it into our existing quality systems,* and some type of document control or ISO process must manage it. Standard work

---

* As Ken Place states, one could argue that without a quality system you cannot sustain one-piece flow as there is no system then available in which to document it. Based on a personal conversation with Ken Place.

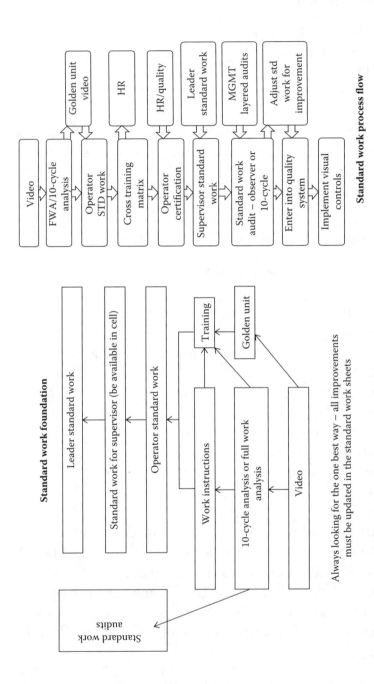

Figure 12.2 Standard work foundation and process flow. (From BIG Archives.)

Figure 12.3 Carl's garage. (From BIG Archives.)

must be audited and then constantly changed as we improve our processes.

Workplace organization is critical to sustaining one-piece flow. If the workbench or office desk is not set up in the proper way, then we will most surely resort back to batching.

5S* is part of workplace organization and helps us to sustain one-piece flow by organizing the workplace to support and, in some cases, mistake-proof the operation so the operator has to do one piece at a time. In addition, customers love a clean workplace. A good friend of mine loves his cars and is a true testament to 5S (see Figure 12.3).

SMED stands for single minute exchange of dies. This means we can do a setup or changeover in less than 10 minutes. In order to do one-piece flow we have to reduce our setup times first, otherwise the long setup times will force us to batch larger quantities. In fact, if you try to reduce the lot size to one-piece before you do SMED you will most probably

---

* Five S (5S) stands for Sort, Store, Shine, Standardize, and Sustain. 5S is part of workplace organization and means a place for everything and everything in its place. It is a combination of good housekeeping and the discipline required to put things away each time.

miss all your customer required delivery schedules. In the next chapter we explore this concept further as we discuss the reasons why we all feel we have to batch.

Without preventative maintenance we cannot keep the equipment running necessary to support one-piece flow. As soon as a piece of equipment goes down, we will end up batching the parts up to just in front of the broken-down equipment.

Will People Pay More for One-Piece Flow?*

A great real-life example of batching vs. flow is thinking about a "cup of Joe" (coffee). How many of you have ever used a 10- to 12-cup coffee maker? How many times have you thrown out at least half a pot of coffee because it was overcooked, cold, or left over from the day before? The whole time you think … what a waste! However, you are stuck with that batch type of system/process. Today, one can purchase a Mr. Coffee 12-cup coffee maker for a seventh the price of a Keurig system. A Keurig system makes coffee one-piece flow. It can even be hooked up to a water line so no manual refilling is necessary. Being seven times more expensive, why has the Keurig system had such success? According to Boston.com,† Keurig, which started in 1998, has now grown into a billion-dollar business. Keurig's commercial models are now in 13% of American workplaces. One out of every four home coffee makers sold in the United States is a Keurig.

In 2010 Keurig sold more than $330 million worth of brewers, which go for anywhere from $79.95 to $249.95 each. The company's real money, though, comes from its "K-Cup" coffee capsules—it sold well over $800 million worth per year.

---

* This Keurig section was inspired by Mike Bland.
† http://www.boston.com/business/articles/2011/08/07/
  the_inside_story_of_keurigs_rise_to_a_billion_dollar_coffee_empire.

Keurig's One-Piece Flow Advantages

- We no longer have to throw out half a pot of coffee.
- Customers can brew a cup of coffee, switch the pods out, and make a cup of tea right after without having to clean the pot or the brew basket.
- The pods are self-contained, so it's easy to switch between coffee, tea, and hot chocolate, and everyone gets their favorite hot beverage.

The company was founded by coffee lovers who wanted to enjoy the same quality and consistency of coffee enjoyed in their favorite coffee houses. From a single question, "Why do we make an entire pot of coffee when we drink only a cup at a time?" came the Keurig one-piece flow system that brews a perfect cup of coffee in less than a minute.*

But in the end, are people really paying more for one-piece flow? Coffee is expensive, and how much waste was involved in the old 12-cup coffee maker process? You may argue the K-Cups are more expensive, but one can purchase a K-Cup reusable filter where you add the coffee to the filter and eliminate the waste associated with the K-Cups. Interestingly enough, Keurig introduced their 2.0 model, which could brew up to 30 oz of coffee at a time. Hmmm. It, of course, uses a much bigger K-cup. This coffee maker was not well received due to a new system that only allows people to use Keurig K-cups and eliminated the reusable filter. They quickly reversed course based on the consumer backlash and are redesigning the coffee maker to be compatible for any K-cups.†

---

* http://www.coffee.org/a-brief-history-of-keurig, note that two parts of K-Cups can be recycled, and there is also a manual cup that can be filled with coffee with no plastic waste. http://homeguides.sfgate.com/kcups-recyclable-79359.htm.
† http://fortune.com/2015/05/07/keurig-coffee-pods-backlash/.

Engineering Changes in a Batch System

Most engineering organizations also tend to batch. Many times revisions to drawings or other documents will wait until a batch of them is ready to be processed. Engineering tasks may be handed out over certain time periods, i.e., "period batch." If the factory is batching and engineering changes the revision, then the batches have to be sorted out. If the factory is doing one-piece flow, then engineering change requests (ECR) tend to have minimal impact, unless their suppliers are batching.

The Human Factor of Why We Batch

I know what things you've been thinking while reading this, or things you will hear when you try to implement one-piece flow yourself. If I had a nickel for every time I heard these following phrases, I could retire:

- We don't have time to implement one-piece flow now. We need to get all our delinquent product out first, then we can look at implementing it.
- You just want us to be robots!
- You guys are crazy! What do you mean you want me to do these one at a time?
- I would have to pick up this tool each time.
- I retire in one year. Do you really have to start this initiative now? Why don't you wait until I retire!
- If I do these steps one at a time it will take forever.
- There is no way you could do this one-piece flow the way we are set up now. It just won't work.
- Every time we turn around we get another engineering change or another specification that "Sales" says we can meet; we can't even test for it! Thank goodness the customer can't either!
- I thought you wanted me to do this efficiently.

- There is no way it could be faster than how I am doing it.
- I don't care if you think it takes longer, this is the way I am going to do it! If you want, you can do it one-piece flow.
- The parts never pass the tester so if we make a cell we will be down and everyone will be idle. This way we can all keep making product (inventory).
- OPF will lead to more mistakes. Besides it forces the operators to work as a team and they don't want to do that.
- I would have to walk over there each time to set it down.
- I don't have room to lay all this out in a line. By the time I do, I could be done.
- If I am doing this operation on one, isn't it more efficient just to do it on the rest? That way I have better quality and won't miss a step.
- We always do it this way.

The fact that these basic, fundamental responses are so engrained in our thought patterns is the main reason why developing a one-piece flow culture is so difficult and ultimately, the reason why so many companies fail.

At another company, we watched curiously as an operator proceeded to disassemble a part instead of continuing the assembly operation. When we asked him why he was tearing the part down, he said it had been assembled by someone else and, frankly, he did not trust that person ... this was a 250-piece batch lot of production! He was averaging 2 to 3 minutes to take each one apart and rebuild it, prior to moving forward with the rest of the operations. No one in management even knew this was going on. We found it occurred over and over again as people were moved around from cell to cell. Does this happen at your company? Would you even know if it does?*

---

* This example came from the *Lean Practitioner's Field Book*, Protzman, Kerpchar, Whiton, Lewandowski, Grounds Stenberg © 2015 CRC Press.

One-Piece/Person Flow

One-piece or one-person flow is always faster, in comparison to processing things, information, or people in batches. Converting from batch to one-piece flow reduces cycle times by reducing extra steps and delays in the process and, hence, reducing the inventory needed within the process. As we implement one-piece flow, it immediately highlights waste, variation, and opportunities inherent in the process, showing clearly what is occurring at each step.

Near our house, there was a construction project just starting, consisting of four new two-story office buildings. The traditional way to approach the project, as cited in an earlier chapter, would have been to do the foundation for each building, and then the first floor for each building, then the second floor, and then the roof, etc.

This developer, however, employed the one-piece flow methodology. After the first foundation was poured he started on the first floor of the first building while pouring the foundation for the second building. Then he worked on the second floor of the first building while working on the first floor of the second building while pouring the foundation for the third building. He then started the roof of the first building and, in parallel, started the foundation for the fourth building and so on.

If, for example's sake, each step took a week, using the old method, he would not have finished the foundations for four weeks. However, this way his first building was complete in four weeks, and he could start renting it out right away. In the old method it would have taken 13 weeks before he could have had the first building completed and started receiving cash. This increased his cash flow by nine weeks.

Batch vs. Flow Example

When we brought up the second line at a certain company, I asked the production manager if he had noticed more output now, compared to when he was batching. He said he didn't really see much difference. I was extremely disappointed in his response. Then he said, "But you know … we only ran it with two people." I asked him how many he normally used and he said, "between three and four people." The manager didn't consider this reduction of labor as an obvious improvement to output!

One-Piece Flow vs. Small Lot

We were staying in a hotel in Columbia, SC, when a bellhop saw me waiting for the elevators around 11:00 a.m.—"checkout time." Much to the chagrin of his front desk supervisor, he said to me, "You know, if they would just stagger the checkout times, the waits for the elevator wouldn't be so long." I told the person he was absolutely correct and saw the front desk supervisor look at him with an angry smirk.

However, it's not his fault, or his boss's, since that was the hotel policy. Most hotels are set up like this.* This is another example of systems thinking.

Many companies and departments have similar strategies as the hotels. They schedule processes to occur at the same time each day, week, or month. For example, we work with many plants that run 24 hours. Do you think they stagger shifts, or have everyone come in at 7:00 a.m., 3:00 p.m., and 11:00 p.m.? Do you think there's ever a race to get to one of four showers, or a long line at the clock-in/clock-out station? Whenever we batch up processes or systems, we automatically invite all of the problems associated with batching.

Fact: As we stated earlier, but cannot emphasize enough, with one-piece flow we will always get the first piece completed significantly quicker than batching. One-piece flow

---

* This example came from the *Lean Practitioner's Field Book*, Protzman Kerpchar Whiton Lewandowski, Grounds, Stenberg © 2015 CRC Press.

reduces cycle times, inventory, and storage time. It also high-lights waste in the process.

Parallel Processing vs. Batching

The key is to understand, in the long run, that anything high volume runs one-piece flow or multiple pieces in parallel (i.e., traffic lanes).

Many times, companies mistakenly feel they are performing work or steps in parallel when in fact they are still batching. For example, if I am working on two hamburgers at the same time, I put out both rolls, grab each burger one at a time, and put each on a roll. Then I put lettuce on each roll, then tomato on each one, next comes the ketchup on each one, and then mus-tard on each one, etc. This is "batching," not working in parallel.

Parallel Processing

If two of us are each working on the same piece, at the same time, then we are working in parallel. Traffic lanes run in par-allel. Running in parallel means I can run multiple products, at the exact same time, through the process or operation. Many high-volume food and beverage production lines run this way. If 10 donuts are loaded at the same time across the conveyor line, and all are fried in hot oil, then coated with icing, then cooled, etc., at the same time, this is parallel processing.

In reality there is a batch of 10 donuts being processed, "segmented batch," in a small "lot" flow. This is one rea-son why we refer to one-piece flow or small lot production. Small lot can also refer to companies that have customers that require very small order quantities. In this case, the company is frequently changing over from one order to the next.

The one-piece flow production system was created to address exactly this type of production. An example would be building subassemblies in parallel to meet up with a final assembly unit. However, if we end up with more than one waiting for the final assembly, then we are batching.

On a side note, how often do you get on a 50-mile-per-hour road only to have to stop at every red light? If you are reading this book and are in traffic management, please time the stoplights to keep the flow going! So much time and fuel is wasted in the United States due to our inefficient transportation systems. In Europe, with the exception of some highly populated downtown areas, there are traffic circles at almost every intersection so cars can continue to flow, saving time and precious fuel. High-speed rail systems cut the travel time in some cases by 80% vs. the highway.

Note:

■ Single-lane roads are one-piece flow.
■ Highways (with no traffic lights) are flow with parallel lanes (until you get too many cars).
■ Traffic lights are batch. Batches of cars go through while others wait.
■ Traffic circles are flow. If designed correctly, traffic keeps moving.

Exercise: You need three to five people to do this exercise and several rolls of quarters. Batch exercise directions: Have one person at each table open one roll of quarters. Have that person take six quarters and turn them each over, one at a time. Then pass them to the next person at the table who repeats the same and so on. (You can vary the lot size or add more quarters, fix or vary the length of time, etc.) Write down the times for

1. First piece completed.
2. Total throughput time—total time to get one piece all the way through (which in batch is the same time as first piece completed).

3. Last piece completed—same as total time for the exercise.
4. Cycle time—will be the total time divided by the number of quarters. If you use 10 quarters it is easy to calculate.
5. WIP.

One-piece flow exercise: Start with one person at each table who takes each quarter, turns it over and then immediately pass it to the person next to them who turns it over and so on. Write down the same times as above and compare them.

You can also turn this into an "innovation" exercise by asking the class … How can we do this faster? Tell them it can be done three to four times faster and they can use anything in the room to help them out. But, tell them each coin must be turned over as it passes them. They will have blank stares and then start thinking. Eventually they figure out to tape all the quarters together and turn them over one, in parallel, and then pass them on to the next person who turns them over once and so on.

Debrief question: Ask them what did they learn?

Another Example of Parallel Processing

When boarding a Southwest plane in Burbank or an Alitalia flight from Turin, we could board both ends of the plane at once using stairs because they didn't have the jet ramps in place. However, people were so programmed to load from the front of the plane that only a few boarded through the back of the plane. Delta boards all their international flights through two entrances. Sometimes, capital-intensive "systems" like the jet ramps get in the way of more efficient loading operations.

Timeout 11

Pull out your batch list again. Look it over. How many of your examples could you convert to one-piece flow (see Timeout 11)?

Timeout Exercise #11

- Pull out your batch list again from Timeout 5. Look it over. How many of your examples could you convert to OPF?

I. _____

II. _____

III. _____

IV. _____

V. _____

VI. _____

VII. _____

VIII. _____

IX. _____

X. _____

The Gray Area between Batch and Flow: Group Technology

Group technology* is a tool used to identify the processes and characteristics necessary to produce each part. We then look to categorize the products into families or similar/like "groups," or services, based on those process steps or product characteristics or profiles. The next step is to create a cell composed of machines, or process steps, arranged in the order that supports the sequential building of the family or parts. The next step is to process the parts through the cell using one-piece flow, or small lots, noting that every part may not hit every process step or machine.

Group technology falls in the middle, somewhere between batching and one-piece flow, and generally leads to segmented batch processing.

An example is having cells set up that produce a family of parts, using the same tooling with a limited number of parts and tools; thus, we can now run the cell with no setup time impact.

■ Take note that, over time, this matrix must be updated; especially in small-volume high-mix machine shops, as machines and customer requirements change over time. The first sign is when a part in a family has to leave the cell to run on another machine in another cell. This is known as "cross-cell processing" and results in batching the parts up to transfer them to the outside cell. The more "cross-cell" parts required, the sooner one needs to revisit the families and update them. There will always be parts that don't fit any product family, and normally we create what we call a "model shop" cell to handle such "misfit" parts. This means some parts

* *Introduction of Group Technology*, John L. Burbidge © 1975 William Heinemann.

will always have to be made in different cells or across multiple cells no matter what families are created. This is where COBACABANA (Control of Balance by Card Based Navigation) can be used.* COBACABANA is a method of using a card system to schedule production, which is different from a traditional kanban system.

Even on very quick operations and machines, one-piece flow tools facilitate the continuous improvement process. This company uses high-volume serializing machines. Even though their operators were only spending 8.75 s in labor time on each card, using the one-piece flow tools we were able to reduce the time to less than 3 seconds.

We have used this tool very successfully in surgery departments. Using group technology, we can calculate exactly how many and geographically what rooms to dedicate to each service line. We then arrange the equipment and materials at point of use near the appropriate service line.[†]

True Mixed-Model Sequencing

True mixed-model sequencing is working "true one-piece flow" *regardless* of the type of product. An example in the automotive industry is when any model type can be produced,

---

* *COBACABANA Control of Balance by Card Based Navigation, An Alternative to Kanban in the Pure Flow Shop*, Dr. Matthias Thürer, Dr. Mark Stevenson, Charles Protzman © 2014. COBACABANA is designed to achieve the same leveling of workload to capacity that is achieved in repetitive manufacturing using Lean tools, but it does so while allowing the company to offer highly customized products to its customers. It reduces the variability of the incoming workload that results from product customization, rather than limiting variation in the product mix itself (Thürer et al., 2014b).

While COBACABANA was developed for job shops, it can also provide an important control alternative to *kanban* systems in pure flow shops with high variety in demand and processing times. See www.workloadcontrol.com.

[†] *Leveraging Lean in Surgical Services*, Kerpchar, Protzman, Mayzell © 2015 CRC Press.

one behind the other, on the same line. This requires the line to be level-loaded. Level loading is the concept of averaging out the demand for daily production. For instance, suppose we make 10,000 Corollas, working 20 days a month, with a breakdown of 5,000 sedans, 2,500 hardtops, and 2,500 wagons. This means we have to divide the total per month by the number of working days. So, 5,000 sedans divided by 20 working days would equal 250 sedans per day. Applying the same logic to the other models would result in 125 hardtops and 125 wagons made daily. Once we have the daily production calculated, we must determine the sequence for building on the production line. The line could be arranged on the production line as follows: one sedan, one hardtop, then a sedan, then a wagon, and so on.* This example shows how the production line at is finely tuned, as each day they are planning for the next several days, the next several weeks, as well as production a few months out.

Timeout 12

Pick a process, any batch assembly process, that has about 5 minutes of labor and is running with one or more persons. Calculate the average cycle time by dividing the total time for the batch and dividing by the number of pieces produced (see Timeout 12).

Then, set the process up (as a pilot) for one-piece flow. Get every part or piece of paper in the right order, make sure there are no reasons forcing you to batch, and then assemble the item one-piece flow. Record the cycle time and compare it to the batch process.

What were your results? What did you observe with each system?

---

* *Beyond Large Scale Production*, Taiichi Ohno, Toyota Production System © 1988 Productivity Press.

Timeout Exercise #12

- Pick a process, any batch-assembly process, which has about 5 minutes of labor and is running with one or more persons. Calculate the average cycle time by dividing the total time for the batch and dividing by the number of pieces produced.

  C T = Total time/Number of Pieces Produced

  _____ = _____ / _____

Timeout 13

One-Piece Flow Exercise

We start with assembling a group of people—normally four to six works best, but groups can be larger. Start with a batching example. The only tools you need are paper, a pen or pencil, a stopwatch, and a flip chart or white board. The paper can be cut up into small sheets.

1. Batch: lot size of 10
   Have the first person in the group write their first and last name on a sheet of paper. Then repeat this on nine more sheets of paper. Then the first person passes the 10 papers to the next person who writes their name on each one. Meanwhile the first person starts another batch of 10. Follow this pattern for 4 minutes. When the first paper is completed, record the time. At the end of 4 minutes, have everyone stop and count how much WIP there is in the process. Any piece of paper not completed with writing on it is considered WIP. Now count up how many were completed through the process. Record the following for each run:
   - Number completed
   - Number of WIP
   - Time for first piece
   - Observations anyone has of the process or the work area
2. Rerun the simulation with batches of five and record the data.
3. Rerun the simulation with one-piece flow. Instead of writing your name on 10 pieces or five pieces, write it on one and pass it along. This is the equivalent of a station-balanced line. Note: work will stack up in front of the slowest person or person with the longest name, and the person after that will be idle.

Timeout Exercise #13

• Follow the exercise on page # ____ and list your findings. Think of a way you can relate this to your own practice. When doing this exercise with others, explain it in terms of your own system for the best possible results. Remember, the more realistic, the more chance of buy-in from your fellow employees.

_____
_____
_____
_____
_____
_____
_____
_____
_____
_____
_____
_____
_____
_____
_____
_____
_____
_____
_____
_____
_____
_____

4. Rerun the simulation with "bumping." In order to bump, the last person in the simulation creates the "pull." Whenever they are finished, they pull the work from the person next to them, regardless of whether or not they have finished. There will be a temptation to want to finish the name before passing it, but this is not allowed. This means the person pulling will have to know how to write the person's name he is pulling from. The last person then completes that person's name and then completes his or her own and pulls again. Everyone in the assembly line follows this process. If a person finishes their name but no one has pulled from them, then they continue to write the next person's name and the next person's name until it is pulled from them. This means everyone has to be cross-trained to fill out each other's names prior to starting the simulation. Normally this requires some practice rounds fist.

In each case the results will improve; from batching 10 to batching five to one-piece flow to bumping. Bumping represents true synchronous balance one-piece flow. Most one-piece flow companies think they are "there," when in fact they are only at the station-balanced level. Bumping will deliver another 10% to 30% increase in productivity in most cases (see Timeout 13).

What Is Bumping?*

As described in the exercise, bumping is the passing of the part from operator to operator based on a "pull" system (see Figure 12.4). It was first described in Ohno's book,

---

* For further information see the *Lean Practitioner's Field Book*, Protzman, Kerpchar, Whiton, Lewandowski, Grounds, Stenberg © 2015 CRC Press.

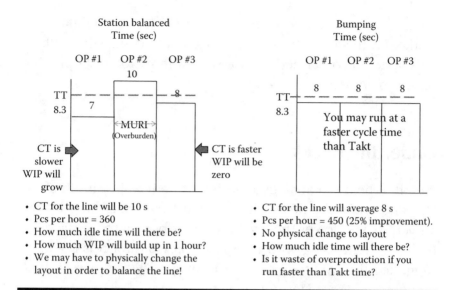

Figure 12.4 Bumping vs. station balancing. (From BIG Archives.)

*The Toyota Production System.** Ohno uses a sports example to explain it.

The station-balanced approach is like a swimming relay handoff. The swimmer on the block has to wait for the swimmer in the water to touch the wall before diving off the block. The bumping analogy is to that of a baton relay race. The runner has a certain zone in which the baton has to be handed off. Th[ɪ]e second runner starts to run before the first runner hits the zone. Then somewhere in the zone it is handed off. Imagine if there was a line in the zone where the handoff had to take place. What would happen? Both runners would have to stop in order to hand off the baton.

We create these same baton zones or what we call flex zones in the layout. The workers can hand off the part anywhere in the zone. In extreme cases of variation, it is possible

---

* *The Toyota Production System*, Taiichi Ohno © 1988 Productivity Press.

for an earlier worker to complete a part before the final worker. In this case, the earlier worker would start the pull. This system is described in more detail in my other book, *The Lean Practitioner's Field Book*.

Under the Rocks

We often hear the analogy that implementing "just in time" (JIT)and one-piece flow is like lowering the water level in a river. As you lower the level the rocks pop to the surface. In fact, Jordan Jiang, who wrote the foreword for this book, suggested the we title it *Batch Thinking—The Submerged Reef on Our One-Piece Flow Journey.*

Think about it for a minute, what are the typical rocks that come to the surface or, in Jordan's words, the reef that comes to the surface? We find many of the following problems submerged in batching environments:

- Design problems
- Parts shortages
- Testing problems
- Problems found in the specs
- Quality problems
- Setup times for assembly lines or machines in the lines
- Worker cross-training
- Tons of WIP that have to be worked off before we can start one-piece flow
- Line balancing issues
- Equipment problems
- Machine breakdowns

We could go on and on with examples. Excess inventory is hiding all these problems.

Batching vs. Flow: What's in It for You to Abandon the Batching Paradigm

For those of you we've convinced, welcome to the new world of endless possibilities and the beginning of your journey in the never-ending pursuit of finding the "one best way." What's in it for you is a big improvement to your bottom line, increase in cash flow, increased inventory turns, better on-time delivery, increase in morale, better safety record, less defects, increased customer satisfaction, and the list goes on.

Chapter 13

Are You Ready for One-Piece Flow?

Are You Ready for One-Piece Flow? A Case Study

Process variation is the bane of one-piece flow. There are times when processes simply are not capable, because of the variation in the process or in the design of the product, of achieving one-piece flow in the short term. It stands to reason that process variation must be understood with solid root cause analysis and then, like a weed, pulled up from the roots. By product variation we are not talking about options to the product but variation within the process itself. The most effective tools we have at the early stages of combating process variation are

1. Standard Work
2. Workplace Organization (5S)
3. Setup Reduction (SMED)
4. Total Productive Maintenance

Most times a layout based on the process flow of machines and assembly can be accomplished concurrently with these tools. It is left up to the business owner, operations manager, manufacturing engineer, etc. engaged in the continuous improvement to determine if the time, risk tolerance, leadership support, capital, and knowledge are all present in the culture to implement one-piece flow all at once. The downside to erring on the cautious side—of not going for the touchdown (one-piece flow) in one play—is the economic opportunity cost. However, as we all know, there will be tangible financial and customer service-level benefits to implementing the four tools above, even if we don't go for the whole enchilada at once.

As an aside, if you fall into the category of accomplishing one-piece flow in stages, you are in the auspicious company of Shigeo Shingo, a renowned Japanese consultant who taught thousands of Toyota team members. He recommended a stage of stability utilizing single minute exchange of dies (SMED) before implementing a sequence of layout improvement, mistake-proofing and source inspection, one-worker to multiple machines, jidoka (autonomation*), and, finally, level loading, over the course of a year.

The authors had just such a decision not too long ago at a company one of us had purchased. It was a classic company turnaround situation. The company designs and manufactures machinery for an industrial market sector. Several of the company's nonfinancial fundamentals were solid. The market perceived its customer service and product quality as solid. The employees were skilled and the culture had a healthy respect for safety.

The company was also a candidate for an industrial version of A&E Channel's show, *Hoarders*.† I honestly believe nothing

---

* Jidoka means automating with a human touch or stopped whenever an abnormality occurs. In English we call it autonomation, as there is no direct English translation.
† http://www.aetv.com/hoarders.

had been thrown out for 15–20 years. Excess and obsolete (E&O) inventory was everywhere, but "it might be able to be used sometime." The culture had not been trained to see the cost in moving the E&O inventory twice before an order could be built. There were seven nonfunctioning microwaves, "in case we ever wanted to use them for parts," for the lunch-room. I could go on and on, but you get the idea. In short, beyond the regular monthly pickup, we have thrown out an additional 18 overflowing dumpsters in the past six months from a 20,000 sq. ft facility. Workplace organization in the form of 5S simply did not exist; and we still have quite a ways to go on our one-piece flow journey.

Standard work, from the management level to the floor, was terribly deteriorated. Like many clients, one could see that many years back this wasn't the case, but now the concept seemed to be lost. There were drawers upon drawers filled with scrap paper and business cards, representing everything from phone inquiry notes to addresses for vendors.

The authors Mike Rother and John Shook describe the term "go see" scheduling in their book, *Learning to See.** All planning and purchasing were done via "go see," which would not have been bad except for the fact they didn't go and see until they needed the part. All too often, the part was missing and prevented a machine from shipping, sometimes for weeks or even months, which then triggered a "go see" by several others before being confirmed missing and turned into a "go purchase" while the machine sat idle. If we could have sold "searching for parts" as a commodity, we would have been in the Fortune 500; but instead, it was just non-value-added activity continually increasing our costs.

Visual management practices were virtually nonexistent; setup reduction and preventative maintenance were equally anemic.

---

* *Learning to See: Value Stream Mapping to Add Value and Eliminate MUDA*, Mike Rother and John Shook, foreword Jim Womack, foreword Dan Jones © 1999 Lean Enterprise Institute.

We needed to decide if we were going to create a one-piece flow assembly and/or fabrication process. I assessed the cultural environment described above and other critical priorities of the business. For example,

- The resurrection of sales and marketing,
- The multiple sources of process variation, and
- The fact that my coauthor would need to get back to his consulting business in two to three weeks.

If one-piece flow were going to succeed, then I would need to devote 80% of my time to it for a year. In a turnaround, cash flow is king, and my time was a scarce resource. Building sales and marketing and the resulting backlog had to take priority. We compromised from one-piece flow and put in a pull system (kanban) between fabrication and assembly. As the saying goes, "if you can't flow, pull."

Let's be clear: we chose to have more inventories as a result of the kanban, which is both cash expenditure and one of the eight forms of waste. We all know the goal should be to eliminate it. However, the weighted importance of the cash-generating effect of orders/sales took precedence and proved to be correct. In the end we proved not to be ready for one-piece flow, even though it is the ideal state.

What are some other impediments to flow or "batch elimination?"

- *Product designs* that require "feel" during assembly. These typically involve functions like tuning or shimming. We have seen this firsthand with electromechanical pressure switches. I recently walked through a factory in which a "seasoned" team member was listening to the internals of a motor while holding a screwdriver on the motor and the other end on his ear. Remarkably, the manager told me he was always spot-on and never allowed a bad product to be shipped.

∎ *Physical separation* was mentioned earlier as a major, if not the primary, cause of batching. I was the general manager of a business that had two buildings at the same location. We managed to put all functions of management and all value-added steps in one-piece flow for a high-mix and rather physically large product line (value stream) in the outer building. Despite repeated analysis, we could not justify the capital to duplicate the entire shipping docks and office in the outer building. We batched the product to take it over to the first building to the shipping department instead.

∎ *Size of the part*, either too large or too small, may have us think we can't do one-piece flow. This falls under variation. Large products tend to result in what we call bay-builds, where everything—the labor, material, and tools—is brought to the bay, where the product is staged for completion. As with all of these impediments, "to thy own self be true"; don't use them as an excuse. If you ever find yourself using this excuse, just keep in mind that Boeing moves 737s through their plant in one-piece flow.

∎ *Equipment or processes that lend themselves to batching*, which may not justify the capital to change to flow. Vacuum furnaces, heat-treating, curing ovens, washing machines, sterilization equipment, etc., all come to mind.

∎ *Shared resources*, which cannot be in two places at the same time. This often takes the form of a machine in which more than one value stream utilizes it.

∎ *Monuments* that cannot be moved can impede one-piece flow and encourage batching or outsourcing. Processes like anodizing and painting are great examples.

∎ *Low volume–high mix* tends to result in people thinking they can't do one-piece flow. However, we find most of the time that this is not the case. Most parts follow a common flow, even though they are high-mix parts. This is where we utilize a group tech matrix to see if we can sort products into families and then set up the equipment and processes in one-piece flow fashion to support each family.

In determining if you are ready for one-piece flow, don't use the aforementioned impediments as an excuse. All of them can, and have been, overcome. The world is one of limited resources of time, skill, and money. The decision to employ pull, or one-piece flow, around an impediment should be based solely on whether the resource can be employed to greater effect elsewhere to maximize the value of the business.

Transitioning to a Flow-based Culture

Once you decide the flow-based culture is right for you and your company, you must now embark on the challenge to transition the culture. In order to make this transition, the company must go through what we call the change equation* (see Figure 13.1). The journey through this equation is a critical process in which every change, whether personal or professional, must pass.

Notice there is a multiplication sign between each letter, because if any of the letters are zero or are not addressed, we will not overcome the R_{change}, which stands for resistance to change, thus effective change will not occur. In addition, each step needs to be followed in order.

C = Compelling Need to Change

The C stands for the compelling need to change. This is more than simple dissatisfaction with the current environment.

---

* See *The Lean Practitioner's Field Book*, Protzman, Kerpchar, Whiton, Lewandowski, Grounds, Stenberg © 2015 CRC Press.

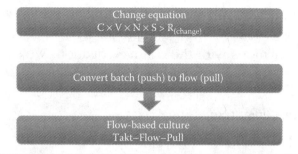

Figure 13.1 Transitioning to a flow-based culture. (From BIG Archives.)

Shigeo Shingo, a consultant to Toyota who trained over 3,000 engineers, stated, "Dissatisfaction is the Mother (relationship) of all improvement." "We feel dissatisfaction," by itself, is not a strong enough statement. People can be very dissatisfied but, for one reason or another, never change. Change is extremely difficult, especially transitioning from a batch-based culture to one based on flow. How many times do I find people who like to constantly complain; yet they are so comfortable with the old way, they refuse to change? If we don't have a compelling need to change, then all efforts are futile and, ultimately, nothing will change. If change does occur and it is not driven or supported at the highest levels, there will be no chance of sustaining the new flow-based processes.

In order to be successful, we need more than just "dissatisfaction" with the way things are today. We have to have so much passion that we "eat, live, and breathe" the change. There are two ways to incentivize change. One is to have an actual "crisis" or business case that, without change, the organization will not survive. The crisis dictates the true compelling need to change. The other way is to invent a crisis, or to set very high goals for the organization that can't be achieved by doing it the way it has always been done. This creates a healthy "fear," or paranoia, that keeps the organization changing/improving. While this can be done at a department level, it is most successful when started at the most senior executive level. Companies tend to go through stages synonymous with the change equation. We call these stages

1. Complacency/regressing
2. Denial
3. Chaos
4. Renewal/revitalization

The biggest problem with success is that it leads to complacency. It is easy to be stuck at complacency for years. Our first nature is to deny it. Once we accept it and decide to kaizen or change (for the better), then there is normally some chaos incurred due to the change process. Then the company updates the standard work and incorporates the change. The true use of the change equation is to always be going through it in order to avoid complacency. One could equate this to the plan do check act (PDCA) cycle. This is where the healthy paranoia comes into play. You have to work on creating the constant need to change and evolve in order to avoid complacency.

Paul Akers, founder and president of FastCap LLC, states, "The idea of doing one-piece flow is so foreign to people that every second of every person's life, batch work is pulling on them. The only way to counteract that is to first have the knowledge that one-piece flow is more effective. You learn that knowledge, you gain that knowledge by doing a couple simple experiments, by making paper airplanes, or in my case I learned the power of one-piece flow when I was making 100 Laserjambs© at a time, taking 45 minutes to make them.

Then the Lean guys came in from Japan and said you're foolish, you should be making one at a time. I looked at them and said, "you know what, you're an idiot, it's impossible, there's no way you can make them one at a time. My batch work method is the best in the world, look how refined it is," and then they said, "Watch."

In just one week they took a process that was so steeped in waste, where it was taking me 45 minutes to make one Laserjamb© when I made them 100 at a time and they took it to just 7 minutes. "Wow, who was the fool now ... it was Paul Akers."

I learned at that moment, that there was some magical element to making one product at a time, to refining processes so they could be easily accomplished based on the current demand of the customer; if the customer wants 1 you make 1, if they want 10, you make 10, 100 you make 100, but you make them one at a time, inspecting every one as you make them so when it comes off at the end you know you have a perfect product. The problem with batchwork, the overwhelming problem with batchwork is that when you make a batch, and make one mistake, you've made that mistake throughout the entire batch and you have to rework that entire batch. The second problem is you have to expand your work area dramatically because now you have to manage these huge batches as they move around your plant.

There are so many negatives to batch-work, and the positives to one-piece flow are so overwhelming, it almost should take your breath away. When I see people doing batchwork, it gives me a coronary, I want to just die ... unfortunately we're human beings, and I'm predisposed to doing batchwork. I fight and combat that every day with the knowledge that I've seen over and over again OPF working dramatically better, and adding more joy and more purpose to my work than any system I've ever used before.

Why Change?

When faced with this question, our answer is "What is the option?" Ask yourself these questions:

- Can we afford to continue to work with the level of waste in our current processes?

- Have past improvements worked? Remember, all the solutions put in place over the years have gotten us to where we are today!
- Is your department or company world-class?
- Do you want to be world-class?
- Are other departments that you impact satisfied with your performance?
- How many of you are satisfied with your current processes?
- Can your company or department survive in the future? Manufacturing is a dynamic industry; so not changing is the equivalent of regressing, because the rest of the world is moving against you.

The cost of batching goes directly to your bottom line. For example, if you are idle, who is paying for that waste? If you have to search for something, who is paying for that waste? Who pays for all the excess inventory created that just sits around or becomes obsolete? The answer is our customer pays for the waste. Remember, waste adds cost to the bottom line, because the company or government agency is paying you while you are waiting at the Xerox machine, idle, or searching for a part or pencil, or batching up processes. This cost makes organizations less profitable, and when organizations we work for become less profitable, financial managers start looking for bodies to lay off. Hence, the true cost of the batching is ultimately our jobs, which are on the line every day.

V = Vision

"I can't get there if I don't know where I'm going."

The next letter in the change equation is V for vision. Vision is important in the change equation because without a vision, how can you chart a course? If people understand the vision and the change that is required to support the vision, then the change will be easier to "sell" and be adopted, thus reducing the resistance to change. One must communicate the vision of the flow-based culture over and over until people are literally tired of hearing it. Takt–Flow–Pull, in this case, best summarizes our vision:

- Takt stands for takt-time. This is the cycle time required by the process, paper, or product to meet the customer's needs.
- Establishing flow is next. This transition from batch to flow is the most difficult part of the journey.
- The last part of the vision is to establish a system that pulls the product (paper, part, or person) to move through the process vs. pushing the product through the process. Batching is based on a "push" system. This means products are continually pushed from process to process until something comes out at the end, leaving tons of work in process (WIP) inventory in its wake. Flow is based on a pull system. We replenish only the customer products which were sold the hour, day, or week before.

N = Next Steps

The N stands for next steps. Once we have a compelling need to change and know and understand the vision, we need to determine the next steps (not just the first) to get to the vision. These steps come from assessing where we are currently, relative to the vision. If the "roadmap" of how we are going to achieve the vision is communicated and people gain an understanding of it, this will help diminish the resistance to change. Thus we need to create a roadmap to flow for the organization.

S = Sustain

The final letter, S, stands for sustain. Once we have implemented our next steps, we must sustain ongoing improvement.

This is the most difficult step of all. Sustaining is the true test of whether there was a compelling enough reason to change and a sign if the other letters were implemented properly. The change must start with you, the reader, and then each individual involved. Ultimately the only way to truly sustain is with top management leadership and drive (not just support). The leadership must be unwavering and totally committed to sustain and continually foster the compelling need to change and the ongoing transition to a flow-based culture.

Change and What's in It for Me

We developed this tool knowing each employee is going to ask "What's In it For Me?" (WIFM) when challenged with a new initiative. It is important that when we begin to answer this question, it is addressed from multiple perspectives. For example, an office manager is in the middle of a flow-based initiative that will reduce cycle times, which will enable more output with the same or less staff, and for sure no more overtime will be needed. Now, let's look at this from different perspectives:

- Employee #1 is silently concerned that she will no longer receive the five to ten overtime hours per week she is accustomed to; therefore the project will potentially impact her current lifestyle and is perceived negatively.
- Employee #2 is a working parent who has struggled over the past year to pick up her children at daycare; from her perspective, the project is a positive one. We find the WIFM question applies to changes even in our personal lives.

Management has to be ready with the answers that will address both positive and negative impacts from the employees' perspective. If we do not answer this question, employees are left in the dark. They will fill in any gaps not clearly communicated with worst-case scenarios and create or spread rumors that will run rampant in the office and on the Internet. Think about the proverbial call from the school nurse. The nurse leaves a message on your voicemail asking you to call her back. What starts going through your mind? You start to think the worst things that could possibly happen.

It is crucial not only to know the answers to the questions below, but also to be able to frame them in a positive fashion. This should not be difficult if there is a truly compelling need to change. The key to WIFM is to answer the questions below from the point of view of the employees each time they are impacted by the change. What do they really want to know and why? These questions will help communicate to the organization the compelling need to change. We generally suggest scripting answers to the following questions prior to starting the Lean journey:

1. What is the change we are making?
2. Why are we making the change?
3. How will it affect the employee? Now and in the future?
4. How will it affect the company? Now and in the future?
5. What's in it for the employee if we make the change?
6. What's in it for the company if we make the change?

Once scripted, it is important to communicate the answers with the staff in each department prior to rolling out the flow-based implementation. This tool forces the leadership to think through each of these questions. The answers must be compelling enough to support the big C in the change equation. So this means not only do we go through the change equation the first time; but, the CEO must figure out a way to continuously repeat the change equation cycle in order to create a systemic way to drive continuous improvement every day and avoid complacency. He/she must create a system to drive continuous improvement every day.

Timeout 14

Your personal action plan ... Pull out your batch list again. Look it over. What would it take to convert to one-piece flow? What's in it for you if you are successful? i.e., increase in cash flow, decrease in inventory, fewer defects, etc. Please list the actions you plan to take on your journey to one-piece flow (see Timeout 14).

Summary

As stated in the beginning of this book, our purpose for writing it was to give the reader concrete examples of why we batch, when we batch, where we batch, and what it costs our companies in revenue, profit, and employee morale.

When someone comes and tells you they *have to batch*, first ask them a simple question ... "Why?" Our bet is their reason will fit into one of our root causes. In order to get to one-piece flow, you will have to use the PDCA (Plan, Do, Check, Act) cycle to figure out the root cause of the batching, and then solve the root cause. Only then will you get to one-piece flow. This is applicable to some, but not all the root causes but for sure to people's mindsets.

To overcome people's minds is the most challenging task involved in implementing one-piece flow. Each one of us is unique, with different backgrounds, experiences, and paradigms. The good news is we all have the ability to change our minds. For this reason, it is important when arguing the virtues of one-piece flow to always give the person supporting batching a way out. Don't back them into a corner. Educate them, have them read books, watch one-piece flow videos, or go see a company doing one-piece flow.

The first rule of a turnaround or for any company is to survive. This means there has to be some progression from batch to flow. The speed at which one moves from batch to

Timeout Exercise #14

- Pull out your batch list again. Look it over. What would it take to convert to OPF? What's in it for you if you are successful? i.e. increase in cash flow, decrease in inventory, less defects, etc.

_____
_____
_____
_____
_____
_____
_____
_____
_____
_____
_____
_____
_____
_____
_____
_____
_____
_____
_____
_____

flow has to consider the ability of the company to resource and implement the change. One has to first determine the priorities. For instance, Ohno started with kanban (pull system) in their machine shop. Then moved to lining up all his equipment in order of the product flow. Toyota has been on this journey for 60 years now and has had plenty of hiccups along the way. Transitioning to one-piece flow is a journey and we all move at different speeds. However, the faster you can get to one-piece flow, the easier it will be to manage and grow your business. We hope we have convinced you one-piece flow is better than batching and that batching is the real silent killer of productivity. We hope you will be successful on your journey. I know for some of you reading this you are still not convinced. That's ok! Hopefully some day you will "get it." The mind is a terrible thing to waste!

One-Piece Flow Consulting

If you need help converting your processes to flow production, please feel free to contact us at danprotzman@biglean. com or CharlieProtzman@biglean.com. Our company, Business Improvement Group LLC, specializes in training and conversion from batch to one-piece flow processes in both factory and administrative settings in all industries. Business Improvement Group LLC has helped many companies on their CI journey realize significant productivity improvements and saved several companies from bankruptcy, especially during the last recession. We can improve any process whether it be manufacturing or transactional in any industry sector: manufacturing, healthcare, government, or service (i.e., banking, insurance etc.). Please see the appendix for some selected company results. Please visit us at www.biglean.com.

Appendix

Additional Readings

- The Lean Practitioner's Field Book, Protzman, Kerpchar, Whiton, Lewandowski, Grounds, Stenberg, CRC Press, ©2015.
- Leveraging Lean in Healthcare Series, Protzman, Mayzell, Kerpchar, CRC Press, ©2014.
- All I Need to Know About Manufacturing I Learned in Joe's Garage: World Class Manufacturing Made Simple Paperback, William B. Miller, Vicki L. Schenk, ©2004.
- The Shingo Production Management System, Shigeo Shingo, Productivity Press, ©1992.
- Customers for Life, Carl Sewell, Pocketbooks, ©1990.
- Flight of the Buffalo, Ralph Stayer, Warner Books, ©1993.
- Good to Great, James C. Collins, Harper Business Press, ©2001.
- Toyota Production System, Taiichi Ohno, Productivity Press, ©1988.
- Toyota Production System, 4th Edition, Yasuhiro Monden, Institute of Industrial Engineering, ©2012.
- A Study of the TPS from an Industrial Engineering, Shigeo Shingo, Productivity Press, ©1989.
- Non Stock Production, Shigeo Shingo, Productivity Press, ©1988.

- Design of a Period Batch Control Planning System for Cellular Manufacturing, Jan Riezebos, Print Partners, ©2001.
- The Introduction of Group Technology, John L. Burbidge, Heinemann, ©1975.
- Out of the Question: How Curious Leaders Win, Guy Parsons, Allan Milham, Advantage Publishing, ©2014.
- The Happiest Company to Work For! Akio Yamada, Norman Bodek (ed.), PCS Inc., ©2015.
- COBACABANA (Control of Balance by Card Based Navigation): An Alternative to Kanban in the Pure Flow Shop, Matthias Thürer, Mark Stevenson, Charles Protzman, ©2014.

Results Converting from Batch to OFP

The following pages represent a small subset of our initial before and after results realized by companies varying in size from small (less than 25 employees) to Fortune 100 by converting from batch to one-piece flow. Please share your batching stories and results with us on our website: http://www.onepieceflowvsbatching.com.

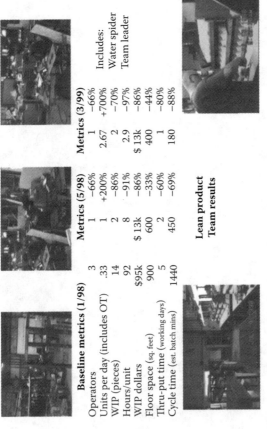

Baseline metrics (1/98)		Metrics (5/98)		Metrics (3/99)	
Operators	3	1	−66%	1	−66%
Units per day (includes OT)	.33	1	+200%	2.67	+700%
WIP (pieces)	14	2	−86%	2	−70%
Hours/unit	92	8	−91%	2.9	−97%
WIP dollars	$95k	$ 13k	−86%	$ 13k	−86%
Floor space (sq. feet)	900	600	−33%	400	−44%
Thru-put time (working days)	5	2	−60%	1	−80%
Cycle time (est. batch mins)	1440	450	−69%	180	−88%

Includes:
Water spider
Team leader

**Lean product
Team results**

Company X results applying design for assembly as part of the Lean tools yielding a 97% increase in productivity and overall labor time reduction of 85%

Source: BIG Archives

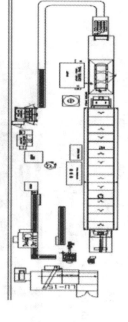

Robotic cell before Lean

Operators	4.5
Output (includes OT)	759
WIP	1,255
DL (min/unit)	3.55
Lathe cycle time (sec)	70
Enshu cycle time (sec)	74.5

Phase 1 actual results

Operators	3	−33%
Output (no OT)	859	+13%
WIP	80	−94%
DL (min/unit)	1.67	−53%
Lathe 1 cycle time	35	−50%
Lathe 2 cycle time	47	−37%

53% increase in productivity

Decreased operator walking dist. 2,250 ft per shift

Freed up one robot and eliminated 2nd shift

Company X: Robotic cell improvements. Decreased operator walking dist. 2,250 ft per shift

Freed up one robot and eliminated 2nd shift

Source: Big Archives.

Baseline metrics (1/98)		Metrics (5/98)		Metrics (3/99)		Includes:
Operators	13	7	−46%	6	−54%	Overhead reduction
Units per day (includes OT)	2.3	5	+117%	5	+117%	
Labor hours per unit	52	9.3	−82%	8	−85%	Water spider
WIP (pieces)*	29	13	−55%	13	−55%	Team leader
WIP dollars	$ 45k	$ 26k	−42%	$ 26k	−42%	In line welder
Floor space (sq. feet)	3,275	2,456	−25%	2,456	−25%	
Thru-put time (working days)	20	3	−85%	3	−85%	Parts not stocked
Cycle time (est. batch mins)	240	80	−67%	80	−67%	

85% increase in productivity – 9× return on consulting fees
All Lean implementation costs paid back well within first year
Teams pick up activities normally associated with overhead

Company X: This company improved productivity by 85% after three iterations.

Source: BIG Archives.

Baseline metrics–station balanced

Operators	3
Units per day per person	12
Paid minutes per unit	120
Thru-put time (working days)	5.5
Cycle time (min - est. batch)	41.9
Overtime #hours estimate per week	15
Space (sq. ft)	728
Travel distance (ft)	257
WIP #	324

Actual after Lean metrics

Operators	2	.3%
Units per day	35	65%
Paid minutes per unit	27.42	77%
Thru-put time	.5	89%
Cycle time (min)	12.2	70%
Overtime #hours	0	100%
Space (sq. ft)	728	0%
Travel distance (ft)	52.4	77%
WIP #	65	80%

77% increase in productivity

Note: The team leader's desk and all the raw materials were added into the cell where the space was freed up.

Company X: This cell used to be 30% on time to their customer—once we fixed all the variation and standardized the process they are now 100% on time to request date with significant improvement to productivity.

Source: BIG Archives.

Before

Operators	7.5
Units per day (includes OT)	1
DL per unit (hours)	60
WIP	50
Thru-put time (hours)	149
Cycle time (hours) est.	8

After actual

Operators	2	−73%
Units per day (includes OT)	1	0%
DL per unit (hours)	16	−73%
WIP	2	−96%
Thru-put time (hours)	6.5	−96%
Cycle time (hours)	6.5	−18%

17% savings using vendor managed inventory (VMI), 55 transaactions to 5
73% increase in productivity = $423,000 contract savings
13× return on consultant fees

Company X: This company received more contracts by exceeding their customer's expectations for on-time delivery, quality, and overall process control for chemical detection equipment.

Source: BIG Archives.

Before

Operators	3
Units per day (includes OT)	69
Output per hour per person	2.5
DL hours per unit	0.4
Floor space (sq. ft.)	2,500
WIP	Lots
Thru-put time (working days)	35 days
Cycle time (sec) estimated	1,327
Distance traveled	10 miles

After actual

Operators	1	−66%
Units per day (includes OT)	62	−104%
Output per hour per person	6.5	+160%
DL hours per unit	0.153	−61%
WIP	0	−100%
Floor space (sq. ft.)	504	−80%
Thru-put time	554	−99%
Cycle time (seconds)	554	−56%
Distance traveled (feet)	42	−99%

- Eliminated need for production facility 10 miles away
- Freed up and sold capital equipment
- Significant reductions in inventory in first six months
- Reduced headcount through attrition
- Reduced factory labor overhead
- Reduced setup times from 3 hours to six minutes
- Some investment was required

Annual savings = better than 10×
Consulting fees
61% increase in productivity

Company X: Weld cell: They used to refer customers to their competitors. We then cut 38 weeks late backlog to 2 weeks early—in 8 weeks. Now they are leaders in market share in their industry.

Source: BIG Archives.

Accounts payable Lean implementation

Baseline metrics: 3-way match process		Actual after Lean metrics: pay by invoice process		
Operators	2.33	Operators	< 0.5	78.5%
Units per day avg	93	Units per day	93	0%
Mins per unit	14.2	Mins per unit	2.6	81.7%
Thru-put time (working days)	11	Thru-put time (working days)	11	0%
Cycle time (mins)	6.45	Cycle time (mins)	2.6	59.7%
Overtime #hrs per day	2.5	Overtime #hrs	0	100%
Space (sq. ft)	286	Space (sq. ft)	64	77.6%
Travel distance (ft)	590	Travel distance (ft)	0	100%
WIP #	1048	WIP #	930	11.3%
81.7% increase in productivity				

Company X: Accounts payable transactional process 81.7% productivity improvement. Freed up 1.8 operators and the AP supervisor. No one was laid off.

Source: BIG Archives.

2pc flow with 2 pc buffer 3-21-03

Operators	4
Units per hour	26
DL mins per unit	9.2
Thru-put time (min)	33
Cycle time (est. batch min.)	2.3
Space sq ft	90

20%+ increase in productivity over Batch

After lean 1 PC flow 3-28-07

Operators	3	25%
Units per hour	33	+25%
DL mins per unit	5.4	−41%
Thru-put time (min)	5.4	−84%
Cycle time	1.8	−22%
Space sq ft	18	80%

41% increase in productivity over 2pc flow

Company X, Casting results, OPF yielded a 41% improvement.

Source: BIG Archives.

2" and 3" motor line 10-18-10

Baseline product flow

After Lean flow

Baseline metrics (not including shafts or pack)

Operators	5
Cell Lead	1
Units per day	40
Paid minutes per unit includes OT	79.2
Thru-put time (working days)	4.42
Cycle time (min - est. batch)	10.13
Overtime #hrs/day	4.8
Space (sq. ft)	5167
Travel distance (ft)	813
WIP #	528

Actual after Lean metrics Nov 2010 data

Operators (eliminated 2nd shift)	5	0%
Cell Lead	1	0%
Units per day	80	100%
Paid minutes per unit	30.8	61%
Thru-put time (working days)	.93	79%
Cycle time (min)	5.03	50.03%
Overtime #hrs	0	100%
Space (sq. ft)	1,640	68.3%
Travel distance (ft)	318.5	60.8%
WIP # (until UV cure is enacted)	75	85.8%

Company X: Yielded a 61% increase in productivity and was able to eliminate overtime and the entire second shift

Batch baseline metrics

Operators	13
Units per day (includes OT)	35
Hours per unit	2.97
WIP (pieces)*	46
WIP dollars	$ 36k
Floor space (sq. feet)	4,000
Thru-put time	63 min
Cycle time (est. batch)	11.4 min

After Lean metrics

Operators	8	–32%
Units per day	35	+0%
Hours per unit	1.82	–35%
WIP (pieces)	7	–85%
WIP dollars	$ 11k	–69%
Floor space (square feet)	2,500	–38%
Thru-put time	3.6 min	–94%
Cycle time (mins)	11.4 min	–0%

35% improvement in productivity

Company X: This company improved productivity 35% by transitioning to one-piece flow and freed up 38% of their floor space.

Source: BIG Archives.

Contact Information

Please contact Charlie or Dan Protzman directly to learn more about their services:

- One-piece flow (Lean) training
- One-piece flow Implementation for Manufacturing, Healthcare, Government, or Service Industries
- Speaking engagements
- Products and services

Charlie Protzman   Dan Protzman
Business Improvement Group LLC
Towson, MD 21286
410.984.1158   443.463.5353
charlieprotzman@biglean.com danprotzman@biglean.com
Website: www.biglean.com

Other books by Charlie Protzman:
The Lean Practitioner's Field Book and the Shingo Prize–winning *Leveraging Lean in Healthcare* series. These books can be found at CRC Press (http://www.crcpress.com/search/results?kw=protzman&category=all) or Amazon.com.

Index